The generation gap has long bee
so I am extremely glad that some
such detail and honesty. A remind
understand other points of view.
- Diane Simpson, consultant promer, writer and speaker
(Silent Generation)

Trying to navigate such a multigenerational workplace is relatively new, and this book offers insights and practical tools to reduce conflict, boost communication and embrace generational differences. Insightful, accessible and incredibly useful.
- Dr Lynda Shaw, behavioural neuroscientist and advanced leadership mentor (Baby Boomer)

Thoroughly engaging and well researched, this book is a fascinating tour of the ages. As well as providing clear insights as to what makes each age group tick, it offers practical advice and easy-to-follow guidance on how to enhance communication between generations. Alastair Greener shows us that empathy, flexibility and tailored communication are the keys to harmony across the ages, which is essential in our increasingly multi-generational workplaces.
- Graham Jones, programme director for undergraduate business degrees, University of Buckingham (Baby Boomer)

If knowledge is power, then this book will supercharge your communication and connection with people older and younger than yourself. With just enough detail to enlighten but not overwhelm, Alastair Greener shows us why we are who we are, and how an understanding that other people might be different is the basis of better relationships, improved communication and a well-functioning society.
- Graeme Codrington, lead researcher at TomorrowToday Futures Institute and author of *Mind the Gap* (Gen X)

Written with warmth, clarity and insight, this book goes beyond stereotypes to reveal what truly shapes each generation and how we can better understand and connect with one another. Alastair Greener's research-backed strategies are hugely valuable for leaders and communicators looking to bridge generational divides and foster stronger, more inclusive cultures. A timely and practical guide for anyone navigating the multigenerational realities of today's workplace.

> – Justine James, partner at Prophet and founder of talentsmoothie (Gen X)

A thoughtful read with a fresh perspective on generational differences in the workplace. It's given me better insight into what each generation values, making me a more effective and empathetic leader.

> – Kristine Long, digital leader, global technology company (Millennial)

This book is filled with myth-busting data and actionable strategies that every person needs, not just every leader. It has fundamentally changed the way I approach all my relationships, both professional and personal. A masterclass in bridging the generation gap.

> – Adam Pickles, head of marketing (Millennial)

Generational insights, brilliantly explained.

> – Tom Penketh , local councillor (Gen Z)

A nuanced and enlightening read about the realities of a multi-generational work force and the truth behind many generational stereotypes.

> – Sophie Abraham, law student (Gen Z)

Author's note

I am very optimistic about emerging generations and the role they will play in shaping our world in the future; however, there are many disadvantaged youngsters who need extra support to help them thrive. So I have set up the Generationally Speaking Foundation which will donate £1 from the sale of every physical book to charities who provide that support in so many important ways. Find out more at the dedicated page on my website: **generationallyspeaking.co.uk/foundation**

Generationally Speaking

How to bridge the generation gap
and communicate with confidence

Alastair Greener

Generationally Speaking

ISBN (paperback) 978-1-915483-94-2

ISBN (hardback) 978-1-917490-19-1

eISBN 978-1-915483-95-9

Published in 2025 by Right Book Press

Printed in the UK in November 2025

Manufactured by
Sue Richardson Associates Ltd.
Studio 6,
9, Marsh Street
Bristol
BS1 4AA

info@therightbookcompany.com

EU Safety Representative
eucomply OÜ
Parnu mnt 139b-14
11317 Tallinn
Estonia

hello@eucompliancepartner.com
+33 756 90241

Contents

Foreword

Deborah Hale MBE

I recall a planning meeting for the London 2012 Olympic Torch Relay when we pondered telling the story of what the torch saw. Not just the stories of those that carried it, but what the torch observed as it traversed its 70-day, 8,000-mile journey. In my mind's eye, I pictured a photomontage where everyone, no matter who they were, what their age was or where they were from, held the same expression on their face. We wanted to see pride, joy, that collective feeling that you are part of something. Our 'moment to shine' – which, incidentally, was our strapline.

I guess that's what we're all looking for, whoever our audience is. That moment of connection and engagement. The moment when our story becomes part of your story. Thirteen years on and the world is a lot more complicated. And yet the opportunities to connect and engage have never been greater.

Whether you are a leader, a marketer or an educator, *Generationally Speaking* is a must-read to help you navigate the current and complex world we need to communicate in.

We are living in an extraordinary moment in human history. We have eight generations alive at the same time, so we are surrounded by an unprecedented diversity of experiences, world views and communication styles. Advances in digital technology also means that the ability to identify, segment and target is greater than it has ever been. And four of the eight generations are still in the workplace. Just imagine if we could properly harness all of this life experience.

In *Generationally Speaking*, Alastair Greener provides a thoughtful analysis of each generation living today and their preferred communication styles. He emphasises the richness of having so many generations coexisting but rightly highlights the fact that the past 100 years has seen seismic shifts in technology, culture and society. So while labels provide an easy shortcut to 'packaging up' a generation, the truth is much more complicated. Greener urges the reader not to fall into the trap of stereotyping – using labels as shortcuts that flatten the complexity of individual lives.

Equally we ought not to simply look through the lens of our own formative years. An important truth in the book is that we must meet others where they are, not where we were. This means acknowledging the context that shaped each generation - and appreciating that this context is not universal. A teenager today navigates the world dramatically differently from the one their grandparents came of age in.

Harnessing the power of the multigenerational workforce we are so fortunate to have requires a real appreciation of what each different person brings. In my own experience, great thinking and complex problem solving happens best when you have a diverse team and a broad range of age, experience, talent and passion. And part of that success is enabling individual contribution and acknowledging the impact on the whole.

As this book so powerfully explores, the key to bridging generational divides lies in communication: curious, compassionate and conscious communication. It requires moving beyond lazy assumptions, listening deeply and finding the shared humanity that exists between someone born in 1920 and someone born in 2020.

The time has come to move past generational labels and toward generational learning. After all, we are not defined by when we were born - we are defined by how we choose to understand and value each other.

Whether you are a marketer hoping to connect with a broader audience, a manager seeking harmony in a multi-generational team or simply someone trying to connect more meaningfully with the people around you, *Generationally Speaking* offers the insights to guide you.

Let this book be a call to action for stronger intergenera-tional appreciation and respect. And with that the opportunity to create the moments and memories that matter and therefore resonate and remain in our lives.

Introduction

'That's so typical of your generation...'

It's a phrase I hear bandied about constantly and it is this kind of labelling which, although natural, is actually very unhelpful when it comes to communication. I remember growing up with another phrase – 'in my day...' – and promising myself I wouldn't use it when I got older. Although I try to stop myself, I can't help it. It's normal to compare ourselves with other people – it's human nature to put yourself in the shoes of a younger generation and recall what it was like for you when you were their age.

In writing this book, my main goal is to help generations understand each other better and help bridge the generation gap in the workplace, at home and in our communities. Much of the friction between generations usually stems from communication or, more importantly, the lack of it. Then there is what I call the 'Generation Blame Game' – which I considered as a title for this book. This is where generations see the negative side of other generations without looking at nuances and the whole picture. This can perpetuate generational stereotyping, which is something I'm keen to avoid throughout this book and in my consultancy work. Not only is it unhelpful, it can also cause misunderstandings and sometimes – even worse – friction.

I was born in 1963, which makes me a Baby Boomer – or a 'cusper', to be exact – although I identify as Gen X. If you don't know what all of that means, don't worry. You certainly will as you read this book. If you already know about the generations – or think you do – then I hope you will find a more detailed, more helpful and more nuanced way of thinking about them through these pages. The results of the two surveys I have conducted will reveal a better picture of how different generations think and communicate. You'll find these results in Section 3, so get ready to be surprised. By picking up this book you're already one step closer to appreciating the eight generations alive today, as well as their differences.

I worked in the cruise industry for 16 years, overseeing the onboard entertainment on 14 different ships. Cruising is a wonderful multigenerational holiday for families to come together and enjoy each other's company in a floating resort. Depending on the itinerary and length of cruise, I would regularly see five generations of the same family sailing together, from babies all the way up to the oldest passenger I ever sailed with, an Australian gentleman who was 106 years old. On board there are activities for every age group, satisfying a multitude of interests, so it's the perfect place to watch the different generations interact. This was the beginning of my interest in generational thinking, because I found it fascinating watching how people behaved towards each other in this unique setting. My job was to ensure all our passengers, regardless of age, were entertained – not an easy task, I can assure you!

Today, as well as supporting organisations to bridge the generation gap through more effective communication, I run a communications training company, Present Yourself, where I help people communicate more effectively in person, online and on camera. I often work with large companies to guide the writing and delivery of their presentations. I also help them prepare their speakers for conferences and assist with corporate messaging and media skills.

It's a varied job and one of the contracts I have is teaching public speaking skills to secondary school students aged between 11 and 18. I've been able to see how the generations have evolved with the increase, and now decrease, of mobile phone use on school premises as well as the immense impact of the Covid-19 pandemic. Until recently, the students have been Gen Z, but it was exciting to see Gen Alpha starting at secondary school in 2023 as another era began.

This work seemed to naturally evolve into a growing interest in generational communication. As well as seeing family, friends and my clients grapple with generational differences, I am intrigued by the misconceptions each generation has of others. This has been fuelled by the stereotypes portrayed in the media and online. I could see the tensions growing because of the lack of understanding. The assumptions many of us make about each generation have created unhelpful labels that cause even more misconceptions.

The first book I read on the subject was *Mind the Gap* by Graeme Codrington. First published in 2004, it was one of the earlier accessible books on generational theory, especially within a workplace and global context. I read the updated 2012 edition, which is still a good read today and a fascinating look at that period before Gen Z were even born. As Codrington suggests, it was and still is a generational rollercoaster. The book made me look at generational thinking in a whole new way.

This led me to research the subject further and the yearning to find out the facts behind generational communication. This led to me commissioning two studies through my communications training company Present Yourself. In the first, the Generations in the Workplace Study 2023, 110 HR professionals responded to a survey and gave their insights into workplace communication. I wanted to see how generational differences influenced people's thinking and the impact this had on the organisations where they worked. I'll talk about that more in Chapter 11, which looks more specifically at the four different generations in the workplace.

The second survey looked at how different generations actually communicate compared with the generally accepted view. My Communication Habits and Preferences Survey 2024 asked more than 4,000 people to say how they liked to communicate in 2024 and included people from all socioeconomic groups. The survey asked questions covering all age groups and this included many areas of communication. Few surveys in the past have covered such a widespread reach and even fewer have focused so much on the UK. You'll find an analysis of the results in Section 3 of this book.

Both studies were carried out by the renowned survey company Dynata and we deliberately didn't disclose to the participants the full details of why we were conducting the survey. They were both labelled 'communication surveys'

because I didn't want people to respond with any precon-
ceptions. As a result, the studies have given me a fascinating
snapshot of generational thinking in 2024.

What you'll discover from this book

My goal is to help you as a reader of this book to develop
and refine your understanding of each generation, based
on the findings from my research. On my mission to reduce
generational misunderstandings, my focus is on communication
that looks at the ways in which people from different age
groups interact and communicate with each other and, equally
important, how they communicate with other age groups. This
is particularly important in the workplace, where my aim is to
create more generational cohesion, and I talk about specific
strategies organisations can consider in Chapter 20. This
follows feedback from HR professionals, who made it clear in
the Generations in the Workplace Study 2023 that generational
communication was an issue in their organisations. You'll be
able to read more about that in Chapter 17.

However, this book isn't just for leaders and managers. It will
benefit everyone in the workplace regardless of their position.
That's because it is about breaking down generational silos and
helping everyone to have a greater understanding of each other.

In this book I also want to help you understand where
patterns exist, where they have been exaggerated and where
they don't. There is an element of myth-busting where I
deliberately delve deeper into some of the assumptions we
often make about each other. This has led me to believe that we
need to be thinking more individually about people rather than
just as a cohort of any particular generation.

You'll discover that although we are all individuals, there
are patterns that are common to each generation. However,
these patterns will vary throughout the world as each country's
historical key moments impact the different generations. This
book looks at major world events with a particular focus on
the UK. An event in one country, such as war or a change of
political direction, will have a greater impact on that country
than others. The events of 9/11 were felt throughout the world,
but mostly in the US where the attacks took place. Every year,

Gallup produces its World Happiness Report and in 2025 Finland was seen to be the happiest country for the eighth year in a row, while the UK and US continued to slip down the table. This will add nuances to shared characteristics, values and communication styles. This is highlighted by my Five Circles of Generational Influence model, which I introduce in Chapter 3.

In Section 1, I'll look at the principles of generation theories and the value of understanding them in the workplace as well as at home and in social situations. Section 2 looks at understanding each generation alive today and what has shaped them, such as the technology they grew up with, as well as musical, political and social influences, with an extra focus on the four generations in the workplace right now.

Then in Section 3, I'll look in detail at the results of my two surveys to understand people's communication preferences and how they are perceived by HR professionals. You'll certainly be quite surprised by some of my findings. In the last chapter in this section (Chapter 19), I compare the results of my surveys with the accepted views of each generation to see how stereotypically we all communicate. This will help you understand the degree to which we are indeed framed by our generation as opposed to being defined by it.

Finally, in Section 4, I'll give some valuable pointers on how to use my research and bridge the generational communication gap. Based on my research and findings, I'll share ten practical strategies to improve generational cohesion and create a thriving workplace that will result in better and more effective communication.

By understanding each other better, we will all be able to communicate in a more meaningful way, whether that's at work, at home, in school, among friends or at play. And while patterns are helpful in understanding generational communication, please remember my mantra, which I'll repeat throughout this book, and that is: 'We are framed by our generation and not defined by it.'

Section 1

Generational thinking

1 The power of generational thinking

The word 'generation' is used a lot but what does it actually mean? In this chapter, I'll introduce the idea of generational thinking and give you an overview of the generations alive today.

According to the Cambridge Dictionary, a generation refers to people of about the same age within a society or within a particular family. I believe most people consider a generation along the lines of the definition in the Merriam-Webster dictionary as people born and living about the same time, or the average period of time from one person's birth to the birth of their children. Today a 'generation' often refers to those cohorts who share similar cultural experiences and societal influences. They will typically experience critical life events at the same time and are exposed to particular historical moments which go on to define their lives. Critical life events are those that require major adjustments and are usually regarded in retrospect as unusually formative or pivotal in shaping attitudes and beliefs. Personal critical life events include the death of a loved one, divorce and unemployment, but these kinds of events occur at different times for each of us. Shared critical life events affect everyone at the same time: things like war, pandemics and historic occasions.

Meanwhile, each generation is tending to get shorter because of rapid advances in technology and shifts in cultural norms, which can create distinct experiences for different cohorts within shorter periods. For Gen Zers and Millennials, technology and the digital revolution have significantly influenced their formative years. This technological advancement has also had an impact on older generations as they interact with an increasingly digital world. The awareness of major historical events, economic conditions and significant cultural shifts is more global than ever before. These shared experiences influence attitudes, values, work habits and communication styles, as you'll find out in the chapters that look at the accepted view of the generations.

A little bit of generational history

Human beings have been fascinated by generations for centuries. In fact, ancient philosophers and historians from Greek, Roman and other cultures often commented on generational differences, highlighting the changing values and behaviours between older and younger age groups. People often quote Socrates for criticising the youth of his time for their 'lack of respect and discipline', a sentiment echoed through history by other thinkers, such as George Orwell, who said: 'Every generation imagines itself to be more intelligent than the one that went before it, and wiser than the one that comes after it' (1945). I'm sure this all sounds very familiar!

The formal study of generational differences began in the early 20th century, although according to William Strauss and Neil Howe in their book *Generations: The History of America's Future, 1584 to 2069* (1991), there are generations going back to the Arthurian Generation (1433 to 1460). The study of generations has evolved into what is commonly referred to as 'generational theory', which is defined as the study of how generational cohorts – groups of people born during the same period and experiencing similar cultural, social and historical events – develop distinct characteristics, values and behaviours. This theory helps in understanding how different generations influence and shape society and how they interact with one another.

One of the foundational figures in generational theory

was Karl Mannheim, who in his 1923 essay 'The Problem of Generations' discussed how people born around the same time are shaped by similar sociohistorical contexts, leading to distinct generational groups. After the Second World War, interest in generational differences grew as significant social and economic changes highlighted contrasts between age groups. Researchers began to identify and study specific generations, such as the Baby Boomers (born 1946–1964), who were shaped by post-war prosperity and cultural shifts.

Strauss and Howe are pivotal authors in popularising generational theory. In *Generations* they proposed a cyclical theory of generations, suggesting a repeating pattern of generational archetypes (Prophet, Nomad, Hero, Artist) and their influence on society. Their work laid the foundation for identifying and characterising subsequent generations, such as Generation X (born 1965–1980), Millennials (born 1981–1996) and Generation Z (born 1997–2012).

The US-based Pew Research Center, a non-partisan think tank that informs the public about the issues, attitudes and trends shaping the world, has also referred to the generational cohorts in this way but said in 2023 it had re-evaluated its methods for reporting on generations and acknowledged the limitations and diversity within generational groups (Parker 2023). It emphasised that while generational labels can be useful, they might not always be appropriate or helpful, so the centre plans to use these labels more selectively. It will sometimes group people by more specific criteria, such as the decade of birth or age during significant historical events, to avoid over-simplifying complex lived experiences.

Generational thinking has been widely used by marketers to target their messages and products at particular age groups and can help recruitment consultants have a better understanding of candidates, but making assumptions about generations can be unhelpful, and I'll talk about this more in Chapter 3. Also, the dates defining each generation, not to mention their character-istics, will not always be the same as you look around the world.

Despite the cautionary note, there is still a huge amount we can learn about people of different age groups by looking at the patterns that clearly exist. I will explore each generation in more detail in Section 2, but for now, here's a brief overview.

Who are the generations?

Today the most commonly accepted generational groups are:

Beginning	Ending	Generation name	Length (years)
1901	1924	The Greatest Generation	23
1925	1945	The Silent Generation	20
1946	1964	Baby Boom Generation	18
1965	1980	Generation X	15
1981	1996	Millennials (Gen Y)	15
1997	2011	Generation Z	14
2012	2024	Generation Alpha	12
2025	2037	Generation Beta	12

With eight generations alive in 2025, the characteristics of each vary enormously, along with their communication preferences.

The Greatest Generation
Born between 1901 and 1924
These are the oldest people alive today and most will be more than 100 years old. According to Statista (2025a), there were 722,000 centenarians alive in 2024 but interestingly the figure is projected to be more than 20 million by 2100. Some of this generation were in their teens when the First World War broke out and came of age during the Great Depression, with many of them going on to fight in the Second World War.

The Silent Generation
Born between 1925 and 1945
Sometimes called 'Traditionalists', this generation comprises people who either fought during the Second World War (the very youngest who did so), or were children during that period. The 'silent' part of their name refers to their stoic, cautious and conformist nature and reluctance to speak out against social norms. They are characterised as valuing discipline, hard work and conformity. Often defined by their resilience

and traditional values, they contributed to post-war economic growth and social stability, prioritising family and community while navigating profound societal and technological changes.

Baby Boomers
Born between 1946 and 1964
Growing up in the years after the Second World War, this generation has witnessed significant social changes. Most Baby Boomers are now retired, but rather than sitting back and taking it easy, many still have jobs – in fact, according to Statista (2025b), as of the third quarter of 2024, approximately 12.1 per cent of individuals aged 65 and over in the UK were still employed. Unlike their parents, they are also often active for their age. They are seen as valuing hard work, loyalty and economic stability. Their experiences have been shaped by high birth rates and suburban growth. Like the Silent Generation, they are characterised as prioritising family and traditional values, and they too have experienced substantial technological and cultural shifts. They are often noted for their optimism, work ethic and stabilising effect.

Generation X
Born between 1965 and 1980
This generation witnessed the transition from analogue to digital, including the advent of personal computers and the internet. While many of Gen X are now reaching senior positions and empty nesting, others are looking to retire early – if they can afford to. They are characterised as valuing independence, adaptability and resilience, and have been shaped by economic fluctuations and changing family dynamics. Often seen as adaptable and pragmatic, they combine scepticism with entre-preneurial spirit and work–life balance.

Millennials (Gen Y)
Born between 1981 and 1996
This generation experienced the rise of the internet, social media and economic shifts such as the 2008 recession. Even the youngest Millennials now have a lot of experience at work, with many older Millennials in supervisory or management roles. Many are settling down into long-term relationships

and (if they can afford to) looking to buy their own properties and start families. Having said that, many are delaying these traditional milestones, prioritising experiences, continual learning and personal fulfilment. A 2024 Pew Research Center survey revealed that among Americans who believe there is an ideal age for these events, many consider ages 25 to 34 as optimal for marriage, having children and buying a home (Lippert & Fetterolf 2025). However, a significant portion of respondents indicated there is no specific best age for these milestones, reflecting a shift in societal norms. Millennials are seen as valuing work–life balance, tech integration and social justice. They tend to be recognised for their tech savviness, collaboration and desire for meaningful work.

Generation Z
Born between 1997 and 2011
Although more than half of Gen Z are still in education, this is the generation now entering the workplace. They grew up in a digitally connected world with smartphones and social media. They are characterised by their tech savviness, social awareness and how they value diversity. Shaped by economic instability, climate change concerns and global events such as the pandemic, they prioritise mental health, inclusivity and sustainability in their lifestyles. Noted for being digital natives and for their entrepreneurial spirit, they are driving initiatives towards diversity and inclusion.

Generation Alpha
Born between 2012 and 2024
I call this the AI generation: as they enter the critical age of early teens, they will be maturing alongside AI and will treat the technology in a similar way that generations before them have used social media or, going further back, the telephone. They are growing up with advanced technology, climate change awareness and global connectivity, which is shaping their education, communication and world view.

The generation that comes after Alpha are just being born and have already been named 'Generation Beta'. The first 'Beta Babies' entered the world in 2025. The exact years and the name for future generations may evolve as demographers, sociologists and cultural commentators observe and define the characteristics of this new cohort.

In Section 2 of this book, I will examine the generally accepted traits of each generation, but as I have already suggested, understanding generations is more complex. As you will read in Section 3, my research shows that generational traits are far from absolutes. However, they are a guide to how each generation thinks. In the next chapter, I'll look at why it's so important, and valuable, to understand the different generations.

2 Why understanding generational communication matters

Never in history have there been eight generations alive at the same time, so understanding how each one thinks is critical. Our generation can influence our interactions in various aspects of life, such as work, friendships and family. According to a World Economic Forum report, between 27 and 30 per cent of the workforce in 2025 are Gen Z, so businesses are having to adjust their practices to meet the expectations of different generations (Koop 2021). When we look at the times and technologies that have shaped us, it helps us to understand ourselves and how we are different to others. Hopefully, that then helps to bridge gaps rather than highlighting and criticising them.

This chapter explains how understanding generational perspectives can help us all to foster better relationships and enhance collaboration – whether that's at work, in our friendships or in our family life.

Generational communication at work

According to the 2024 State of Business Communication report by Grammarly, poor communication could be costing companies more than 18 per cent of the total salaries paid – and that cost is incurred year after year. In the report, business leaders estimate poor communication in the workplace accounts for a loss of 7.47 hours per employee per week. Now add in the generational factor and the challenge of communicating effectively becomes greater. In the workplace, there are currently four generations and differences can significantly influence communication styles, work preferences and attitudes towards technology and hierarchy. This will have an impact on productivity within the workplace as well as attrition rates.

In my work running the communications training company Present Yourself, I commissioned some research into generational differences in the workplace. Of the 110 HR professionals who answered my Generations in the Workplace Study 2023 survey, 66 per cent felt communication with and between generations in their workforces posed challenges for their business efficiency. Meanwhile, in the same study, more than 50 per cent of HR managers felt their organisation would benefit from implementing strategies to foster inter-generational collaboration and teamwork. There are more details of this survey and its findings in Chapter 17.

As you will discover in Section 3, each generation often has distinct communication preferences. If you want to connect with a person from another generation or influence their decision making, understanding these differences can prevent misunderstandings and enhance collaboration. For instance, managers can tailor their communication methods to suit each of their team members' styles, ensuring that everyone is engaged and informed. As telephone communications expert Anthony Stears told me on my *Alastair Greener Generationally Speaking* podcast: 'Different generations bring different ideas – mixed-age teams give you better inclusion and creativity.'

This adaptability fosters a more inclusive and productive work environment. Generations differ in the way they like to work, so by understanding these preferences, employers can create more satisfying work environments. For example, offering flexible work arrangements can appeal to Millennials and Gen Z, while providing opportunities for professional development can keep all generations motivated and committed. This tailored approach can lead to higher job satisfaction and retention rates. I'll talk more about this in Chapter 20, where I set out how everyone can thrive in a multigenerational workplace.

When it comes to attitudes towards technology and hierarchy, generational differences in the workplace can be quite pronounced. Younger generations, who have grown up with technology, are often more adept at using digital tools and are comfortable with flat organisational structures. Older generations often prefer traditional hierarchical structures and may need more support to adopt new technologies.

Recognising these differences allows organisations to provide appropriate training and support, ensuring that all employees can contribute effectively. When designing technology adoption strategies, it helps to consider the varying comfort levels of the different generations when it comes to using digital tools. Understanding generational preferences can also aid businesses in attracting, engaging and retaining talent, as well as tailoring their products, services and marketing strategies to resonate with different generational preferences and behaviours. By embracing this level of awareness, organisations could see productivity grow and attrition rates fall.

Friendships

True understanding of generational communication can promote greater social understanding and cohesion by fostering respect and empathy across age groups. Generational differences influence how friendships are formed and maintained. Although it's often natural to seek out social time with people from the same generation, who are more often like-minded, stepping out of your comfort zone will often be rewarded with wider and stronger social connections with differing perspectives. Different generations have varying approaches to social interaction. While Baby Boomers and Generation X often prefer in-person interactions and phone calls, Millennials and Generation Z are more inclined towards social media and messaging apps.

By understanding these preferences, we can all choose the most effective ways to connect with friends from different generations. A Gen Z individual might understand that a phone call can be more meaningful to a Baby Boomer friend, while a Boomer might appreciate the convenience and immediacy of a text message to a younger friend. Recognising these values can help individuals find common ground and appreciate the diverse perspectives their friends bring.

Family life

So often we hear that there is a disconnect between children and their parents and grandparents, with all three generations struggling to understand each other. An article by Gaby Hinsliff in the *Guardian* newspaper in November 2024, for example, looked at the phenomenon of adult children choosing to go 'no contact' with their parents. It delved into personal stories and research indicating that a significant number of families experience estrangement due to reasons ranging from abuse to irreconcilable differences in beliefs, highlighting the profound emotional toll on both sides. This is nothing new – it's always been this way. My 85-year-old mother told me about the arguments she had with her mother when she was 18 and the reaction to her declaration that she was going to emigrate to Australia (she didn't end up going!). There is also often friction between parents and grandparents of a child because of their distinct parenting styles – again, nothing new. By understanding and recognising these different styles, however, parents and grandparents can appreciate each other's approaches and learn from one another. It can also assist in creating a supportive environment for children where they benefit from a mix of structure, independence and open communication.

We can learn so much from each other. I love seeing the children from my local primary school visiting older people in our village care home and seeing how much they all get from each other: the older generations sharing their wisdom and experiences, the children bringing energy and excitement while teaching new technologies and youthful perspectives. This exchange of knowledge and skills can strengthen family bonds and ensure that valuable traditions and modern insights are both cherished and utilised. It also helps in bridging the generational gap, leading to a greater mutual respect and understanding.

We now have a more diverse society and understanding how different generations think is invaluable in so many aspects of life, including work, friendships and family. By recognising and valuing generational differences, individuals can cultivate more inclusive, respectful intergenerational relationships, enhancing both personal and professional interactions – with the added benefit of a more cohesive and empathetic society.

The importance of generational communication continues to grow as the workforce and consumer base become increasingly diverse. By understanding and effectively navigating these differences, organisations and individuals can enhance relationships, improve collaboration and drive success.

Having said all this, in the next chapter I'll explore why we shouldn't make assumptions about how any generation behaves or communicates. I'm going to look at how and why we should focus on patterns rather than putting people into generational pigeonholes.

3 Framed by generations – not defined by them

In writing this book, I didn't want to predict where patterns within generations exist and where they don't – I approached the whole topic with an open mind. I set out to be able to help understand patterns of communication within generations but also study how different people in each generation can vary significantly. In this chapter, you'll learn about my Five Circles of Generational Influence, which will help you understand why these differences exist within generations, but also show why there are generational patterns.

Generations are complex

There are clearly some strong patterns when it comes to generational thinking, as a result of the environment (and history) during the period in which that group grew up. The danger is the tendency to label people by their generation and create stereotypes that are unhelpful. The problem is that it's normal for us as humans to over-rely on patterns. As neuroscientist Dr Lynda Shaw told me, human beings are hard wired to pigeonhole people and viewing people within a generation as the same is our brain's way of saving time and energy. So, while there are clear patterns within a generation, individuals within it don't all behave the same or show the same characteristics.

It's a little bit like reading the horoscopes in a daily newspaper: every Cancerian isn't going to be the same or have the same outcomes at the end of the day. So, we read them with a wry smile and don't take them too seriously – or hopefully not.

Another issue is *when* someone is born within the generational span. For example, if you are born towards the end of a generation, you will also have strong influences of the next generation – which leads to the term 'cusper'. This applies to every generation, with one of the most talked about groups of cuspers being the 'Xennials', referring to people born between 1979 and 1982. Cuspers may identify more with traits in the previous or next generation than those of the one they were technically born into. As you will discover in the results of my survey in Section 3, this particularly applies to younger generations like Gen Z, who are currently at distinctly different stages of their lives, so the communication styles of a 14-year-old and a 28-year-old will have a lot of variations. This makes the whole subject of identifying someone by their generation more complex.

There is a lot more science behind generational thinking and the patterns that exist, such as the work done by psychologist Jean M Twenge. In her book *Generations* (2025), Twenge uses large-scale datasets to examine generational differences in attitudes, behaviour and mental health. She is known for her critical analysis of how technology and cultural shifts impact younger generations. Having said that, it's still important to distinguish the differences between people of every generation.

However, some commentators and experts are pushing back on generational theory, so much so that they talk about 'Perennials', identifying people by a particular mindset rather than a specific age group. The term was introduced in an article called 'Meet the Perennials' by writer and entrepreneur Gina Pell in 2015. The concept of Perennials focuses on people who stay current, continually learn and adapt to new situations, regardless of their age. This approach contrasts with traditional generational labels like Millennials or Baby Boomers, which categorise people based on their birth dates. In his book *The Perennials* (2023), Mauro Guillén suggests: 'The inversion of the traditional organisational hierarchy by age means that most assumptions built in to human resource, talent and career management are becoming obsolete.'

It's a great approach and it certainly can help to break down generational silos, but I think it will be hard to break away from generational bias. My own approach is to accept that there is a lot to be learned from understanding patterns within a generation, while at the same time it's also important to be aware of some important caveats. To illustrate this and to help show how many elements can shape generations and individuals, I created a model I have called the Five Circles of Generational Influence.

The Five Circles of Generational Influence

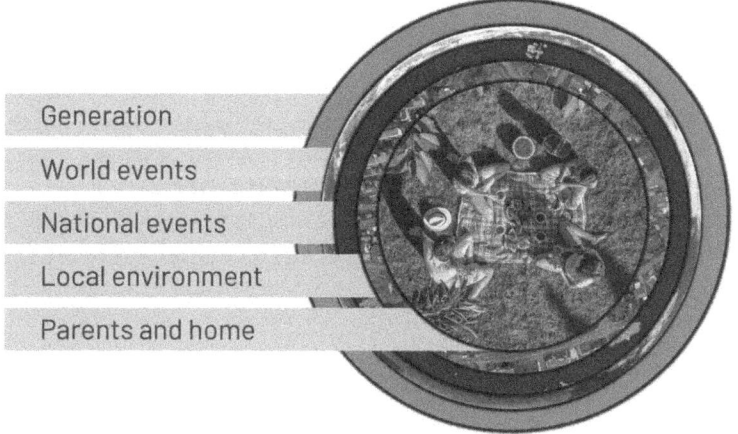

Generation
World events
National events
Local environment
Parents and home

This model examines and illustrates what makes an individual who they are. For each generation, it starts with when they were born, then considers all the influences that exist as they grow up – especially around the formative years between 10 and 14, when the brain is more susceptible to its environment. The first circle represents the generation, then the circles of influence on our character continue inwards to the increasingly individual and personal, moving from world events to home life and family.

World events

While there are events that affect the entire world, such as wars and economic turmoil, the impact will rarely be the same in every country. Although societies are becoming more global, each country is different, so a Baby Boomer growing up in the US will have had quite a different upbringing to someone in the UK. For example, the US was literally booming after the Second World War, whereas the UK had rationing until 1954. War-torn Europe struggled for many years after the end of the war in 1945 as each economy dealt with the extensive damage physically and mentally. This will have had a strong impact on children in each of those countries.

Also, every country has a different economy and indeed their economic cycles will vary in their timing, and this will impact their inhabitants. The financial crash of 2008 was felt very differently in the US, Europe and Asia, so the effect on each of their societies would depend on where you were living at the time. In the United States, it led to significant job losses, with unemployment peaking at 10 per cent (Federal Reserve History 2013). This led to a steep rise in poverty and a major stock market decline, wiping out household wealth. Europe faced bank failures, requiring government bailouts such as those for Northern Rock and Royal Bank of Scotland in the UK, and this led to the region experiencing a prolonged economic downturn. Asia, initially less affected, later saw sharp GDP contractions, export reductions and currency pressures, particularly in countries such as Japan and South Korea. These differences highlight how the effects of the crisis depended heavily on regional economic structures and global interconnectivity. As the world becomes more of a global economy the knock-on effect in one region or country is more widely felt.

More recently, the Covid-19 pandemic was responded to very differently across the globe and this has had a direct impact on each country's population. China enforced some of the most stringent restrictions, particularly in Hubei province, where the virus was first identified. Measures included complete movement control, closure of non-essential businesses and strict stay-at-home orders. In contrast, Sweden adopted one of the least restrictive approaches, opting against mandatory lockdowns. Instead, the Swedish government relied on voluntary guidelines, keeping most businesses and schools open while encouraging social distancing and personal responsibility. Then the rest of the world implemented different levels of lockdown. Even within a country there were marked differences, as there are with many other aspects of life.

National events

Even within a country there are national events that will affect different parts of any country differently. Floods or droughts are often associated with certain parts of a country, having a devastating impact on those living there. Likewise, major sporting events such as the Olympics will be focused on a particular region. Economically, most countries have more industrialised regions and economic turmoil will have a very different impact on regional communities. Then there are those areas that are closer to the financial centre – which isn't always the capital. We often hear about countries with a north/south or east/west divide and this will impact greatly on someone's outlook. But even within a region there are differences.

Local environment

Within a region there will be urban, suburban and rural areas, and where you are brought up will impact with whom you mix as you form your views. According to the Statistical Digest of Rural England, in 2021, 16.9 per cent of England's population lived in rural areas, equating to approximately 9.5 million people (Defra 2025). This suggests that 83.1 per cent resided in urban areas. Some regions and towns are more diverse in their populations than others, which will affect an individual's outlook. The type and size of school someone goes to will also be a key influence.

Parents and home

The UK government's Study of Early Education and Development (SEED) collects comprehensive data on household structures, economic conditions and the quality of parenting and home learning environments in England. Findings from this study suggest that family circumstances and parenting quality are pivotal in shaping children's developmental outcomes, reinforcing the significance of the home setting in early education (Department for Education 2021). This cannot be underestimated, as parents will raise their children quite differently. There will be many factors that affect this upbringing and the home environment, but all will shape an individual's perspective. Even if you are in the same friendship group, your influences won't be exactly the same.

On my *Alastair Greener Generationally Speaking* podcast, I spoke to Claudette, who was born in central Birmingham in the 1970s (making her Gen X) to parents who were part of the Windrush Generation from Jamaica. On 22 June 1948, the HMT *Empire Windrush* brought 492 passengers from Jamaica to the UK. This marked the beginning of what would come to be known as the Windrush Generation, referring to the thousands of people from Caribbean countries who were invited to Britain between 1948 and 1971 to help rebuild the country after the Second World War. With this heritage, Claudette told me on the podcast, 'Growing up in a Jamaican household there were very clear traditions and ideals that we were brought up with.' Her experience was clearly very different to mine growing up on my parents' farm in north Cornwall, and this will have given us a very different viewpoint of life.

Even within the same family, with the same upbringing, there will be differences in personality traits. A study published in the *Journal of Personality and Social Psychology* found that non-shared environmental factors account for variations in personality traits among identical twins (Baker & Daniels 1990). This is because even when raised together, identical twins can experience different interactions, peer relationships and personal events, leading to individual personality development.

Every generation goes through life stages

People often forget that a generation is evolving all the time and never stops evolving. Normally patterns within a generation will not emerge until the individuals within that generation reach their early teens, when they are more aware of influences around them. But of course, that's just the beginning, as they progress through the key stages of life such as university, first job, long-term relationships, children, retirement, grandchildren. Their approach to life will be framed by the key influences that happen along the way. For example, during the

Covid-19 pandemic, we were all at different stages of our life cycle and that affected our experience over those years. As a society, we have seen the impact at every stage of life, from toddlers not being able to interact with other children and gain key social skills all the way up to university students learning remotely and the elderly in care homes not being able to see their loved ones in person. The experience will also depend on which country you were in during the pandemic, with varying levels of lockdown – time will tell how much impact this will have on someone.

Older people sometimes forget that their views of younger generations are seen through the lens of when they were that age. They forget that the youngsters they are judging are growing up in different times and don't act in the same way as previous generations at that age. In the 1960s, people would dress up to go on a plane trip or to the theatre. Those same people have become increasingly less formal over the years in the way they dress and behave. The challenge is that their expectations of other generations aren't consistent with the era those more recent generations are growing up in.

The problems of generational unconscious bias

You will most likely have heard of unconscious bias. It refers to the attitudes or stereotypes that individuals hold subconsciously, which can affect their behaviour and decisions. These biases operate automatically and can influence judgements about others based on factors such as race, gender or age without the person being consciously aware of it.

When it comes to generational thinking, unconscious bias often manifests in the form of age-related stereotypes. Younger people might be seen as inexperienced or entitled, while older individuals might be perceived as resistant to change or less technologically savvy. You will see in Section 3 how wrong these assumptions can sometimes be as they are often made without evidence and can be deeply ingrained in people's thinking. This kind of bias affects all age groups, whether it's dismissing the ideas of a young professional due to their age or overlooking an older worker for a promotion because of perceived obsolescence.

The damage caused by such biases can create real problems in the workplace. Age-based assumptions can lead to discrimination in hiring, promotions and opportunities for development. Younger employees might be denied leadership roles or mentorship because they are not seen as ready for the responsibility or capable enough. Meanwhile, older employees might be overlooked for challenging projects or continuing education because they are wrongly assumed to be nearing retirement or resistant to learning new skills.

Unconscious generational biases not only stifle individual potential but also deprive organisations of diverse perspectives and talents. Age-related unconscious bias in the workplace can perpetuate stereotypes, leading to division and a lack of understanding between generations. This can hinder workplace cohesion, limit opportunities for intergenerational collaboration and exacerbate inequalities.

In Chapter 19, 'Thriving in a multigenerational workforce', I will look more at how organisations can address unconscious bias through organisation-wide awareness and education.

Why socioeconomics affects generational behaviours

Another aspect of generational thinking that needs consideration before putting people into generational pigeonholes is each individual person's socioeconomic background. Working with research specialists Dynata, I tried to ensure that my study on communication habits would have a strong cross-section of UK society and across socioeconomic groups. The reason I was so particular about this is because when data is gathered across a range of socioeconomic groups, it can better show the influences on experiences, values and opportunities that can lead to different generational perspectives. Criticism of survey methods suggests that there is a common bias in research to gather middle-class data and this can result in skewed findings that fail to represent the full spectrum of generational experiences, particularly those of lower or upper classes. This middle-class bias may lead to inaccurate generalisations that do not effectively reflect the views of diverse populations. We hear a lot, for example, about Generation Z's commitment to the environment and how they often make more sustainable choices than older generations. This may be true, but if you are on a low income struggling to pay your bills, you often don't have the same choices. It's important to interview people across socioeconomic groups to ensure an accurate picture.

The result of these caveats is that although I will be talking a lot about patterns, please don't rely too much on them – however tempting it might be. This book will help every reader gain a greater understanding of who we all are, and it will also bring into focus the need to understand the individual. It's OK to see patterns, but when we put people into pigeonholes we create unhelpful stereotypes and sometimes damaging assumptions.

To understand the patterns that we may see among the generations, the next section of this book will look at the accepted view of each of the generations. Understanding these commonly held views can be a useful guide to understanding each generation better. These are not absolutes – just a guide. Because, as I keep saying, we are framed by our generations, not defined by them.

Section 2

Understanding the generations

4 Who are the generations?

In this section, I'm going to look at each generation in more detail, because as Stephen Covey says in his best-selling book *The 7 Habits of Highly Effective People* (1989): 'Seek first to understand, then to be understood.' But first a bit more on what defines a generation, because this can be a big area of debate. For example, the exact dates that each generation spans are somewhat arbitrary. As I mentioned in the previous chapter, experiences can also depend on where in the world you live and the major events that have been pivotal during each generation's upbringing as a result. A good way to look at generations is to think of them as chapters in the story of human progress, shaped by unique events, cultural shifts, technological advancements and economic conditions.

The historical context in which a generation comes of age plays a significant role in shaping its collective identity. World wars, economic recessions, technological revolutions and social movements are just a few examples of events that leave indelible marks on generations. For instance, the Silent Generation, born during the Great Depression and the Second World War, developed a mindset centred on resilience and conformity, while the Baby Boomers grew up in the post-war era of economic prosperity and social change, fostering a spirit of optimism and activism.

Culture and technology are powerful forces that influence

generational characteristics. The rise of television, the internet, social media and now artificial intelligence, for example, has dramatically altered how different generations communicate, consume information and interact with the world. These technological shifts have also contributed to the rapid pace of change between generations, leading to distinct differences in values, work ethics and lifestyle choices.

As the last chapter examined, although it's important to acknowledge that individual differences can exist within each generation, there are certain common traits that tend to emerge. These often reflect the values and priorities shaped by generational context. For example, Generation X is often characterised by independence and adaptability, having grown up during a time of shifting family structures and economic uncertainty, while Millennials are known for their tech savviness and desire for meaningful and collaborative work, influenced by the digital revolution and changing workplace dynamics.

Key influences

Over the next six chapters I will focus on each generation in turn and pick out the cultural and historical events during their formative years. These are the major events that will have affected most people in a generation, such as war, recessions and major developments in technology. I'll highlight the music they liked to listen to, the films they watched, the cars they drove and the technologies they encountered. I'll look at the language they used and where those influences came from, as well as the people they would have interacted with.

There are other common factors that have helped shape a generation to become who they are today. These include major sporting events such as England winning the World Cup in 1966 and London hosting the Olympics in 1948 and again in 2012. Digital technology has been another key driver. For earlier generations, it didn't exist in their youth, but they have had to acclimatise. Most of us have had to learn how to access the internet for mobile banking or use relatively new communication channels such as WhatsApp. Change is generally harder for older generations, who have many years of habits to overcome compared with the more agile-minded youth – but as you'll see in Section 3, we all have to be careful of making assumptions. Some older people clearly love technology, while there are some Gen Z who hate it.

In each chapter, I'll look at one of the generations alive today and what has defined them using a series of headings and focusing primarily on people and events in the UK and US. The idea of the headings isn't to create rigid categories but to give a broader picture of trends and tendencies. I'll start by asking who each generation is.

Who are they?

There are certainly some key characteristics that each generation will have in common as a result of the environment and era in which they grew up. In each of the chapters that follow, you will discover a little more about each generation's levels of independence, resilience and preferences, which in turn shape their decision making and interaction with others. I will also look at the generation of their parents and how that influences their upbringing, as well as the impact of what was happening in their early and formative years.

Notable figures and cultural reference points

Each generation will have been influenced by key individuals who defined the era. Most of us will recognise these people as those who have helped shape our thinking, whether they are from the world of music, the arts, sport, or leaders in business and politics. These are the people each generation will have grown up with or been influenced by, and who have made an often deep impression in their lives. To paint a picture of each generation's aspirations and the culture of the times, I've also included sections on first cars they are likely to have bought (or dreamed of owning) and iconic coming-of-age films.

Young lives

In this section I will look at what was happening in each generation's early years that will have helped to shape their thinking. Having said that, the stage of your life when you are most impressionable is debatable. Some would suggest up to the teenage years, although it has been said that the most crucial milestones in a child's life occur by the age of seven. After all, it was the Greek philosopher Aristotle who is understood to have said: 'Give me a child until he is seven and I will show you the man.' I believe the environment you grow up in and the major events that take place in your childhood, especially just before the teenage years, will have a huge impact on your thinking. In *The Anxious Generation* (2024), Jonathan Haidt suggests there are 'sensitive periods', particularly the years between ages 10 and 14, which are especially impressionable when it comes to influences on people's lives. This period is when the brain is more malleable or 'plastic', meaning people at these ages are more susceptible to what's happening around them. Haidt suggests these are the times when it is easy to learn something or acquire a skill, and that outside these periods such adaptability is more difficult. He illustrates this by saying that language learning is the clearest case. Children can learn multiple languages easily, but this ability drops off sharply during the first few years of puberty. An example of this sensitive period, Haidt suggests, is when a family moves to a new country: the kids who are 12 or younger will quickly become native speakers with no accent, while those who are 14 or older will probably be asked where they are from for the rest of their lives. Personally, I believe the plasticity of learning lasts for a longer period and, as always, you must be careful of generalisations. My second cousin moved to America when he was about 20 and his English accent isn't detectable, but his mother, who was in her 40s at the time, never lost hers.

When it comes to generational thinking, Karl Mannheim suggested in 'The Problem of Generations' (1923) that the *formative years* are roughly the period of late adolescence to early adulthood, typically between the ages of 17 and 25. He considered this to be the time when individuals are most impressionable and responsive to the social, political and cultural events around them. Mannheim argued that it was events occurring during those years that shape a person's world view and collective identity. But given the speed with which young people are growing up in the 21st century, I would suggest this influence starts at a younger age, typically from secondary school, when young people gain more independence.

Education

Styles of education have evolved enormously over the past 100 years, from the formal 'speaking at' style of teaching to the far more interactive learning of today. Certainly, when I go into schools, I barely recognise the styles of teaching. Classroom discipline has changed as well as the teacher–student relationship. Technology has had a big part to play, with the advent of radio, TV, video and interactive whiteboards. Long gone are the days of the ink monitor and blackboards (younger readers will have to do a search to find out what they are!). Meanwhile, higher education has also changed, with 37.5 per cent of 18-year-olds going to university in 2022, according to the UK government (Bolton 2025). This compares with estimates from the same source of just 5 per cent in 1954, an era when the majority of the population went straight into work at the age of 16. This number gradually reduced over the years and then the Education and Skills Act (2008) meant that all young people in the UK should be in education or training until their 18th birthday. The number and types of courses being offered as well as the style of learning in higher education have also changed dramatically. Students during the Covid-19 pandemic had a very different university experience from previous generations when learning went online, along with their contact time with lecturers and professors.

At work

For those generations in the workplace there has been a huge evolution too, especially when you look at the experience of Gen Z starting work. The application process as well as interviewing and onboarding have changed dramatically when compared with the experiences of Baby Boomers and Gen X. Then of course you have the added impact on those who started their first job during the Covid-19 pandemic. While Millennials are generally moving into management roles, the C-suite (an organisation's highest-ranking executive leaders, whose titles typically begin with 'chief', such as chief executive officer, or CEO), is seeing the shift from Baby Boomers to Gen X and older Millennials. Meanwhile, there are so many jobs today that only existed in science fiction 30 years ago – who would ever have thought drone operation would become such a sought-after skill? There are also the jobs that have gone as many Western countries such as the UK have become less industrial and more focused on the financial, technological and service industries. In the following chapters, I'll look at the way in which the working environment has changed and the working experiences of each generation.

The Covid effect

There were multiple factors that impacted each of us when the Covid-19 pandemic struck, and every generation was at a different part of its life cycle at the time. Whether they were at school, university, in work or retired, the experience will have been very different. Although the experience was quite different around the world, such as the levels of lockdown, the pandemic will have had a huge impact on every one of us – though especially the young, for whom those years will have been a greater proportion of their lives. This is why it's understandable that many believe Gen Z, as the coming-of-age generation at the time, would have experienced the biggest and most defining impact. The pandemic clearly had a tremendous legacy for every generation's health, financial stability, social interactions and perspective.

Expectations

We know that people's expectations evolve as they grow older and priorities change. But lifestyles have changed too as many key stages of life, such as marriage, owning a home, having children and retirement seem to be happening later in life. We are also living longer than our parents and grandparents. Long gone for most people is the expectation of three score years and ten (70) as a life expectancy. But there is also resentment from some younger people who see older generations having opportunities they feel are out of reach for them. So, what was each generation's expectation in 2025?

Leisure

The way each generation spends their free time has changed dramatically over the past 100 years, with the ability to travel transforming the way we spend it. According to accountancy firm Price Bailey, in the UK pubs are closing at an unprecedented rate, with a total of 41,000 in 2013 down to 38,175 by 2023 (Bayley 2024), while coffee shops have boomed. According to research commissioned on behalf of the 2018 London Coffee Festival, the number of UK coffee shops has gone up from 10,000 as of 2007 to 24,000 in 2023 (Wholesale Coffee Company 2018). The way we consume entertainment has also been transformed, from families sitting around one television in the house in the 1960s to 2025 when members of the same family enjoy individually streamed entertainment on multiple devices in all parts of the house. This massive variation has made a huge impact on the way we spend our leisure time and how we spend time with one another (see Thompson 2025).

Attitudes to money

The final aspect that I'll look at for each generation in the following chapters is the way they feel about money, debt and saving. These attitudes vary enormously. This is partly due to the stage of life someone is at, but it's also cultural. Each generation has been brought up to view money in different ways and this has helped to shape how they view their finances and therefore their lives. Much of this is shaped by what we see our parents do with their money. It will also be informed by the financial state of the economy as they were growing up – was it during a boom or bust period? This will have an impact on an individual's financial resilience and attitude towards risk.

The influence of individualisation

There is a further influence that has helped shape each generation, and that is individualisation. Rather than relating its influence to each generation individually, it is more helpful to trace how its impact has played out across the span of the generations that I cover. The concept began to gain prominence in the late 20th century, particularly through the work of sociologists such as Ulrich Beck and Anthony Giddens. Beck's 1986 book *Risk Society* and Giddens' *Modernity and Self-Identity*, published in 1991, laid the foundation for understanding how modernisation and globalisation altered social structures. According to Beck, industrialisation brought about the decline of traditional societies, which had been primarily organised around collective identities such as family, religion or community. In their place, individuals were increasingly expected to construct their own identities based on personal interests, careers and consumption choices.

The impact of individualisation has been the breakdown of rigid class and social structures. Going back to the 19th century, people's roles were largely predetermined by birth, class and gender, with little flexibility for personal change. However, as industrialisation took hold, individuals had more opportunities to pursue education, mobility and career shifts. The ability to make decisions based on individual merit and ambition rather than inherited status created space for greater self-expression and autonomy.

Individualisation became more obvious when the post-war Baby Boomer generation became part of a big attitude shift. They were the counterculture generation of their time who in the 1960s and 1970s focused on personal freedom, civil rights and self-expression. This generation grew up during a time of unprecedented economic growth and stability, allowing many to challenge societal norms and embrace a more individualised lifestyle. Boomers were also the first generation to benefit more widely from higher education and economic mobility, leading to increased personal choice in career and family structures. This concept gathered pace for Generation X, who experienced a different wave of individualisation. They came of age in an era of economic uncertainty and rapid technological changes. In his 1991 book *Generation X: Tales for an Accelerated Culture*, Douglas Coupland explored the characteristics and cultural dynamics of Generation X, characterising them as the first to fully embrace the 'self-made' ethos. He suggested that they often felt the need to balance independence and self-reliance with the desire for personal success in a competitive environment, leading to a strong sense of individualism and adaptability. The rise of dual-income households and a decline in traditional family structures during this period also contributed to a sense of independence.

Millennials have seen the impact of individualisation through different lenses. They were raised with the idea that they could 'be anything' and were encouraged to pursue unique paths of personal fulfilment. Social media and digital culture have amplified this sense of individualism by offering platforms for self-expression. As I'll talk about more in Chapter 8, which focuses on this generation, this was the era when there was a shift from what Jonathan Haidt calls a play-based childhood to a phone-based one. However, Millennials also face economic challenges, including student debt, housing affordability and job insecurity, which have led to more pragmatism. While they seek personal fulfilment, they also strive for stability, often adopting gig economies, freelance careers and other non-traditional forms of employment.

Finally, Generation Z has come of age in a world where individualisation is more embedded than ever. Hyperconnectivity and digital platforms allow them to curate their identities on a global stage, leading to a highly individualised sense of self. This generation is particularly focused on mental health, diversity and inclusion, often challenging traditional norms with even more fervour than previous generations.

While individualisation has encouraged greater personal freedom and autonomy across all generations, it has also created new pressures. The responsibility for success, happiness and identity formation increasingly falls on individuals rather than collective groups, which can lead to anxiety and social fragmentation. Yes, individualisation offers opportunities for personal expression and empowerment, but it can also exacerbate social inequalities by placing more emphasis on personal responsibility, often disregarding the structural forces that shape individual lives.

As I have discussed in this chapter and Chapter 3, there are many factors that will define individuals and generations, but there are enough commonalities that will create generational patterns. It is these patterns that form the accepted view of generational traits. The issue in question will always be to what degree these patterns, and therefore accepted views, are accurate. Section 3 will give an indication of what the picture looks like today and how close the accepted view of a generation is to the feedback given by the respondents in my survey. The next six chapters will look at those patterns and the accepted view of six of the eight generations alive today.

First and last: Beta babies and the Greatest Generation

As the first Generation Beta babies were only born at the beginning of 2025, it's a bit early to predict what their generation will look like, but we do know they will grow up in a very different world to the one we see today.

The other generation alive today that doesn't have a chapter dedicated to it is the Greatest Generation, who were born between 1901 and 1924. Interestingly, two luminaries of this generation were Nelson Mandela (born 1918) and Ronald Reagan (born 1911), who had a dramatic and lasting impact on world politics during the latter part of the 20th century.

The majority of the Greatest Generation still living are now more than 100 years old and represented less than 1 per cent of the world's population in 2024. According to the United Nations' population projections for 2024, the world is home to an estimated 722,000 centenarians but in the same report they predict that by 2054, the global centenarian population will be nearly 4 million. The term was popularised by the American journalist Tom Brokaw in his 1998 book, *The Greatest Generation*. This generation represent an era of unprecedented challenges with the Great Depression and the Second World War, with some growing up in the First World War. They are recognised for their emphasis on duty, community and hard work, which continues to inspire admiration and nostalgia for an era characterised by strength and resilience.

Growing up for this generation was framed by world events and the youngest were only in their late teens at the end of the Second World War, so there were many differences between the attitudes of the older and younger members of the generation. However, this will have been different around the world, depending on their country's involvement in the two world wars and the aftermath, which had a direct influence on this and the next generation. Someone growing up in North America would see the world through a very different lens to someone brought up in Eastern Europe as borders shifted.

Wherever they were in the world, though, this was the generation led a post-war world and was pivotal in the advancements in technology and science of the age, paving the way for the next generation – the Silent Generation, who are the subject of the next chapter.

5 The Silent Generation

Born between 1925 and 1945

According to Statista (2025), just 6.3 per cent of the UK population in 2022 were from the Silent Generation, but although they may be small in number, they have had an outsized impact on the way we live and work today.

Who are they?

Often described as stoic, loyal and understated, the Silent Generation grew up in the shadow of the Great Depression and came of age during or just after the Second World War. Many will have experienced evacuation, wartime separation and mothers stepping into the workforce. They witnessed the birth of the NHS, the rise of television and the early digital revolution that shaped modern Britain.

The term 'Silent Generation' was coined by *Time* magazine in 1951, reflecting this generation's reputation for being cautious, conformist and less outspoken than those that followed. Despite this label, they made major contributions in politics, business and the arts. As parents of the Baby Boomers, they navigated rapid societal change in the 1950s and 1960s. Today, they're typically seen as valuing respectful, in-person and formal communication – reflecting the social norms they grew up with.

Notable figures

Here are some notable Silent Generation public figures. These were the people that were all growing up at the same time, who will have shared experiences.

- **Music:** John Peel (1939), Elvis Presley (1935), Tina Turner (1939), John Lennon (1940), Cliff Richard (1940), Barbra Streisand (1942), Aretha Franklin (1942), Paul McCartney (1942).

- **Acting:** Clint Eastwood (1930), Elizabeth Taylor (1932), Michael Caine (1933), Julie Andrews (1935), John Cleese (1939), Michael Crawford (1942).

- **Leaders:** Martin Luther King Jr (1929), Mikhail Gorbachev (1931), Dalai Lama Tenzin Gyatso (1935), Joe Biden (1942).

- **Business:** Zig Ziglar (1926), Jim Rohn (1930), Warren Buffett (1930), Sir John Madejski (1941), Michael Bloomberg (1942), Sir Martin Sorrell (1945).

- **Sport:** Jack Nicklaus (1940), Bobby Moore (1941), Muhammad Ali (1942), Billie Jean King (1943), Arthur Ashe (1943).

- **Other:** Andy Warhol (1928), Jean Rook (1931), Neil Armstrong (1930), Mary Quant (1930), Ralph Lauren (1939), Stephen Hawking (1942).

First car

For most of the Silent Generation, buying their first car wouldn't have happened until the post-war period and was a significant milestone. However, it was far from affordable for most people. Due to rationing and the economic aftermath of the Second World War, car production was initially limited, and many vehicles were still in short supply. However, as the 1950s progressed, production began to increase. While prices for new cars were relatively high, they were still attainable for the middle class, especially with options for hire purchase agreements, which allowed buyers to pay in instalments. Financing options like these helped to make cars more accessible, though many still had to save up or rely on family support to make their purchase. Despite these challenges, owning a car represented independence and mobility, which were increasingly valued during this period of rebuilding and post-war optimism. First cars would have likely been the Morris Minor (1948), Austin A30 (1951) and 'new' Ford Anglia (1953).

Iconic coming-of-age films

This generation came of age during or just after the Second World War and many of their formative years were influenced by the aftermath of the war, social changes and the rise of cinema as a major cultural force. The films that were particularly impactful for them – which would have only been available at the cinema – reflect themes of resilience, rebuilding, youth culture and post-war life. Iconic films for this generation included *Gone with the Wind* (1939), *The Wizard of Oz* (1939), *Citizen Kane* (1941), *It's a Wonderful Life* (1946), *The Third Man* (1949), *Kind Hearts and Coronets* (1949), *The Blue Lamp* (1950), *On the Waterfront* (1954), *The Dam Busters* (1955), *Rebel Without a Cause* (1955) and *Billy Liar* (1963).

Young lives

Younger members of the Silent Generation grew up during the Second World War, with the youngest being born in its final year and some of the oldest in their later teens at the time, serving in it. Many children of this generation were born during the six years of the war, with some in urban areas being evacuated to the countryside. Many would have seen their fathers going off to war while their mothers looked after the house with limited resources and with many working in factories and on the land. No one growing up in this era escaped the horrors of war, which made it a time of great sacrifice and resourcefulness.

Education

Education for this generation was marked by its formality and structure. It was heavily focused on the 'Three Rs': reading, writing and arithmetic. What marked this generation was that during their childhood in the UK, the 1944 Education Act (also known as the Butler Act) was introduced, which meant free secondary education for all. In the US, the GI Bill provided veterans with access to higher education. This brought a big change, although the emphasis remained in line with previous generations, with a focus on rote memorisation, standardised testing and strict discipline. Subjects such as history, geography and science were also taught and the approach was very structured, with teachers as the primary source of knowledge. Education during this time was characterised by a strict and authoritative environment. Corporal punishment, such as caning or spanking, was commonly used as a disciplinary measure, with teachers holding significant authority.

Students were expected to be obedient and respectful, often with little room for questioning or creativity. Education also depended on your gender, with boys and girls receiving different kinds of training. Boys were typically prepared for careers in trades or professional fields, while girls were often directed towards domestic sciences or secretarial skills, reflecting the societal expectations at the time. Higher education was less accessible than it is today, with fewer people attending college or university. In 1950, only 7 per cent of 17-year-olds were still in full-time education, according to the Office for National Statistics (Bolton 2025). For those who did stay on into higher education, significant social mobility often followed.

At work

How you saw the world in the post-war era depended on where you lived. While the US was booming in the early 1950s, the UK and other European countries still had rationing as they rebuilt their cities and infrastructure. The Silent Generation entered the workplace during this time and in Britain the era was marked by a period of recovery, transformation and modernisation.

The governments of the day implemented a mixed economic

model, with significant state control over industries such as coal, steel and railways under nationalisation. Businesses focused on rebuilding infrastructure and increasing production, aided by investments in manufacturing, housing and energy. Consumer goods industries began to grow, reflecting an improvement in living standards and disposable income.

The 1960s brought a wave of economic optimism and social change, which influenced businesses to adapt to new market demands and cultural shifts. This period saw the rise of consumerism, fuelled by a growing middle class, increased wages and technological innovations. The car and electronics industries flourished, with iconic brands such as Mini. Retail transformed with the advent of supermarkets and the first self-service shops. However, towards the end of the 1960s, the UK also faced the challenge of declining competitiveness in traditional industries. Industrial relations issues affected successive governments and had a great impact on younger members of this generation as they entered the workplace. This was followed by an era of turmoil in the 1970s and 1980s as the Silent Generation became the more experienced members of the workforce.

In terms of characteristics at work, this is the generation of hard work, dedication and loyalty as they were brought up to respect authority. In their book *Generations* (1991), Strauss and Howe suggest that the Silent Generation grew up in a period of strict social order, shaped by the aftermath of the Great Depression and the Second World War. During their formative years, they were influenced by strong authority figures such as parents, teachers and national leaders. These figures often upheld societal structures and formal titles. This upbringing fostered respect for hierarchy and authority, which was reflected in their professional lives. When it comes to communication, the Silent Generation are patient and appreciate it being slower and more deliberate. They tend to be conformists, having lower rates of activism compared with later generations.

Most of the Silent Generation are now retired (in 2025, the youngest are 80 years old), although with better health prospects than previous generations, some are still working. In fact, at the time of writing, Howard Tucker from Ohio is the Guinness World Record holder for being the oldest practising doctor at the age of 102. While few centenarians are still working, there are many examples of octogenarians continuing their careers. David Kershaw is Britain's oldest teacher at the age of 82, having spent more than six decades in education. He continues to be called upon by the Department of Education to assist struggling schools and was honoured with a Lifetime Achievement award at the Pearson National Teaching Awards, recognising his exceptional contributions to education (2024). Then there is John Goodenough, who was born in 1922 and died just short of his 101st birthday in June 2023. He was the oldest ever recipient of a Nobel Prize, winning the prize for chemistry in 2019 when he was 97!

So, why are many of the Silent Generation still working? For some, it may be due to financial necessity, but for most, like 90-year-old Maurice Collins, whom I interviewed on my podcast and is still working, it appears to be the desire to stay active and to contribute. The changing nature of work allows for more flexible and part-time roles, while many older people are self-employed. In Britain, the DIY store B&Q launched its Age Diversity Project in 1990, which focused on an older workforce (HR News 2024).

The Covid effect

The Silent Generation were mostly retired when Covid-19 hit and they faced unique and heartbreaking challenges. As one of the most vulnerable groups, they bore the brunt of both the virus and the measures taken to control it. Travel plans were cancelled, family visits reduced to Zoom calls, and those in care homes endured the devastating isolation of months without seeing loved ones. For many, these restrictions came during their final stages of life, leaving families without closure and individuals feeling lost and often bewildered.

For those who emerged from this time, the pandemic offered a sharp reminder of how fragile life can be. Much like the aftermath of 9/11 in the US, there has been a shift in perspective since, with an apparent determination to seize life's opportunities and focus on what truly matters. Travel, family time and long-postponed dreams have moved to the top of the priority list, driven by a sense of 'If not now, when?'. According to a trend report by Booking.com in 2024, the Silent Generation is seeking to make up for lost time by embarking on trips they had previously deferred. My mother is in her mid-eighties and is seizing on the opportunity to travel while she still can.

For the Silent Generation, the pandemic left a lasting legacy of valuing human connection, meaningful experiences and living life to the full.

Expectations

This generation grew up in an era defined by stability, structure and sacrifice. Their expectations in life were shaped by the aftermath of the Great Depression, the Second World War and a focus on rebuilding and community. For most, like Maurice Collins, their goals were to find a secure job, build a family and contribute to society. Career loyalty was the norm and changing jobs frequently was not only rare but often viewed as risky or irresponsible. With this backdrop, it's unsurprising they might feel perplexed by younger generations' tendency to change careers or pursue non-traditional paths.

For the Silent Generation, life was about doing what was needed and finding pride in a job well done. This led them to value discipline, resilience and respect for established norms. Now, as they look forward, their expectations have shifted. Many now prioritise relationships, meaningful experiences and leaving a positive legacy. They want to spend time with family, pass on their wisdom and enjoy the fruits of a lifetime of hard work. Milestones and family events such as birthdays are treasured and very special. While they may not fully understand the career-hopping culture of today, they can appreciate the broader pursuit of happiness. Speaking to my 85-year-old mother and her friends of a similar age, they may struggle to keep up with the pace of life at times, especially when it comes to technology, but they enjoy looking at the world around them through the eyes of their younger relatives and friendship groups.

Leisure

Leisure time was a rare luxury rather than a given for this generation. Growing up when they did meant that their formative years were focused on necessity, duty and practicality. Entertainment often came in simple, communal forms such as listening to the radio, watching films at the local cinema or enjoying what would have been comparatively modest family outings. Hobbies such as gardening, sewing and DIY projects were not just pastimes but often practical pursuits that contributed to the household.

In the post-war era, time off was valued but seen as a reward for hard work, not an entitlement, with one annual holiday somewhere within the same country. It was only the more affluent who would ever get the chance to go abroad on holiday – that was until the package holiday, which arrived in the mid-1960s, made travel further afield more accessible.

In their later years, leisure for this generation has taken on new meaning. With more time and generally a greater disposable income than their parents, they have become great travellers and the tourism industry is thriving partly thanks to this age group. Although the cruise industry, which I was a part of for so many years, is now more popular than ever with all generations, according to a 2023 report by Cruise Lines International Association (CLIA), 15 per cent of cruise passengers were over 70 years of age, and a good proportion of them would be over 80. While spending time with grandchildren, travelling or engaging in creative hobbies such as painting or writing are popular leisure pursuits, the values of simplicity and purpose are still very much on their minds. They look for leisure time that feels meaningful, grounded and, where possible, is shared with loved ones.

Attitudes to money

Given the era that they grew up in, it's unsurprising to learn that the Silent Generation has always had conservative values when it comes to money, with a strong emphasis on saving. They prioritised financial security, often avoiding debt and focusing on long-term stability. In their earlier years, they were diligent savers, often setting aside funds for emergencies and future needs. As they transitioned into retirement, their financial focus shifted towards preserving wealth to ensure a comfortable lifestyle in their later years. Many still have a frugal mentality, with the aim of keeping funds back for a rainy day. When I invited my 85-year-old mother to come to our village café for a coffee, I was asked: 'Why? We have coffee here, so just come here and save the money.'

Having said that, a notable trend has emerged among some in this generation. It's the inclination to 'spend the kids' inheritance', often referred to as 'Skiing'. The term seems to have been coined in the early 2010s and became common parlance by the end of the decade. A 2019 article by the Royal Bank of Canada (RBC) was titled 'SKI'Ing – Spending the Kid's Inheritance'. Previous generations were keen to leave a financial legacy for their children and younger relatives, but some of the Silent Generation want to spend the rewards of their hard work on travel and leisure activities rather than solely preserving assets for their descendants. Research from travel services provider Booking.com indicates that 40 per cent of the Silent Generation prefer to spend their money on a trip of a lifetime rather than leaving an inheritance. Times have definitely changed!

Summing up the accepted view of the Silent Generation

The Silent Generation came of age during a period defined by economic uncertainty and world wars, and have seen some remarkable technological advancements: television, jet aircraft, space travel, computers, mobile phones and the internet. They've witnessed and experienced some of the most innovative advancements in healthcare and, of course, now the rise of artificial intelligence. Their formative experiences instilled values of hard work, frugality and a commitment to stability. Often overshadowed by the larger Baby Boomer generation, the Silent Generation became known for their caution and conformity, shaped by a 'don't rock the boat' mentality. Their interactions with Millennials and Gen Z can occasionally reflect a cultural gap, particularly around technology and social norms, yet they are often appreciated for their storytelling and grounded advice. In a world that increasingly prioritises rapid innovation and individualism, the Silent Generation offers a reminder of the enduring value of collective effort, patience and resilience.

6 Baby Boomers

Born between 1946 and 1964

I was born in 1963, so I am definitely a Boomer. I'm also a cusper, meaning I'm at the very end of one generation and close to the beginning of another, and feel I have more of the traits associated with Gen X. This does raise the interesting point of which generation an individual may identify with, and as you'll see in Section 3 of this book, this is more nuanced than you may think.

Who are they?

Baby Boomers are probably the best defined of the 20th-century generations, named after the post-WW2 spike in the birth rate that began in 1946. While the biggest birth rate rise was in the US, where it peaked in 1957, the rest of the world was also seeing a large upswing. In the UK, according to the Office of National Statistics, these years saw the biggest birth rate boom since 1919, after the First World War. In the UK there were two booms in the same generation: one in 1946 and another in 1964. The main reason for these increases was the economic growth and increased prosperity that marked the post-war period in many countries. This was particularly the case in the

US, where, according to the International Monetary Fund (IMF), the economy was stronger in the immediate post-war period than those of Europe and Asia (Krueger 2006). The availability of stable jobs and rising incomes allowed families to afford more children. There was also a strong cultural emphasis on family life and traditional gender roles, with many people aspiring to the ideal of the 'nuclear family'. However, in the UK, although the birth rate increased, economic growth would take longer, with rationing not ending for the British people until 1954.

Interestingly, this generation is defined more by the length of the birth rate boom rather than the major societal changes and significant events that would frame later generations. Some would suggest that those born in the early 1960s were too young to experience the counterculture of the 1960s and early 1970s and shouldn't really be considered Boomers. This generation developed massively in their youth, covering the flower power hippies of the 1960s right up to the yuppies of the 1980s.

They were the first to grow up experiencing widespread television and, as young adults, they became the drivers of massive cultural shifts, including the civil rights movement, feminism and anti-war protests. This was the generation that oversaw some of the key law changes around homosexuality, sex equality in employment and abortion. They were very much a part of major cultural moments and changes such as Woodstock (1969), the Stonewall Uprising (1969) and Roe v Wade (1973) in the US, and the Bristol Bus Boycott (1963) and the first Race Relations Act (1965) in the UK. For women of this generation there was massive change with the rise of 'Second Wave' feminism in the 1960s and 1970s, which focused on issues of equality and discrimination. Starting initially in the US, the women's liberation movement, as it was often called, soon spread to other Western countries. This generation, possibly more than any other until Gen Z, challenged authority, redefined societal norms and shaped the modern ideas of freedom and individualism.

Today, Baby Boomers are frequently viewed as a bridge between tradition and change. Now entering or well into retirement, Boomers continue to have a significant economic impact and political power as one of the most politically active generations. They also account for a substantial portion of consumer spending, with over-65s in the UK representing

18 per cent of the population, yet controlling around 50 per cent of the UK's wealth, according to the Office for National Statistics (2021) and the think tank the Resolution Foundation (2022). This is possibly one of the reasons why there is friction between Boomers and younger generations, alongside tensions over differing values, particularly around technology and work–life balance.

The Baby Boomers redefined every life stage compared with previous generations and now, as they age, they are experiencing retirement very differently. With advances in medicine and care, they are having a significantly longer retirement and are busy seeking active, purposeful lives, while continuing to influence the cultural and societal landscape.

Notable people

These are the best-known Baby Boomers who also helped to shape an era of rapid change.

- **Music:** David Bowie (1947), Elton John (1947), Bob Geldof (1951), Michael Jackson (1958), Madonna (1958), Prince (1958), Whitney Houston (1963).

- **Acting:** Arnold Schwarzenegger (1947), Meryl Streep (1949), Robin Williams (1951), Carrie Fisher (1956), Tom Hanks (1956), Tom Cruise (1962).

- **Leaders:** King Charles III (1948), Pablo Escobar (1949), Vladimir Putin (1952), Tony Blair (1953), Barack Obama (1961), Keir Starmer (1962), Kamala Harris (1964).

- **Business:** Alan Sugar (1947), James Dyson (1947), Richard Branson (1950), Bill Gates (1955), Steve Jobs (1955), Tim Berners Lee (1955), Jeff Bezos (1964).

- **Sport:** George Foreman (1949), Martina Navratilova (1956), Björn Borg (1956), John McEnroe (1959), Steve Redgrave (1962), Michael Jordan (1963).

- **Other:** Steven Spielberg (1946), Andrew Lloyd Webber (1948), Oprah Winfrey (1954), RuPaul (1960), Diana, Princess of Wales (1961).

First car

For Baby Boomers in the UK, buying their first car was an exciting milestone, often occurring in their late teens or early twenties, typically in the 1960s or 1970s. While cars were still considered a significant purchase, they were more affordable compared to later decades. According to Retrowow, the average price of a new car in the 1960s was around £500–£700, which, while a stretch for many, was often within reach for younger adults, especially if they had a full-time job. The introduction of hire purchase agreements and financing options also made car ownership more attainable. For many, owning a car symbolised independence, and it was considered a reasonable aspiration given the relatively lower cost of living and stable employment. Most, though, sought out affordable second-hand cars. Although often unreliable, they were easier to repair yourself than current vehicles – especially with the help of keen parents. First cars were often the Triumph Herald (1959), Mini Cooper (1961), Renault 4 (1961), Ford Cortina (1962) and Hillman Imp (1963).

Iconic coming-of-age films

Films for Baby Boomers reflect the societal changes, cultural shifts and personal struggles of growing up during the post-WW2 era. Many of these films, released in the 1960s and 1970s, explore themes of rebellion, self-discovery and love. Movies that will remain etched on Boomers' minds would probably include: *The Sound of Music* (1965), *The Graduate* (1967), *The Italian Job* (1969), *American Graffiti* (1973), *Star Wars* (1977), *Quadrophenia* (1979), *Chariots of Fire* (1981) and *The Outsiders* (1983).

Young lives

So much took place during the post-war era as countries were rebuilding after the Second World War. In the UK, Baby Boomers experienced the benefits of the newly established welfare state with the introduction of the NHS in 1948. They were the first generation in Britain to have access to free medical services for all. They were also the first TV generation, watching programmes specifically targeted at them, while younger Boomers saw rock 'n' roll give way to bands such as The Beatles and The Rolling Stones.

Education

Education for Baby Boomers in the UK saw significant transformation, shaped by the post-war commitment to rebuilding opportunities. With the younger members of the Silent Generation, they were the first generation to benefit from the 1944 Education Act, which made secondary education free and mandatory until age 15. This was the era of grammar schools, secondary moderns and technical schools. While designed to promote equality, the system often reinforced divisions, with grammar schools offering the clearest path to higher education.

Schools expanded rapidly to accommodate the baby boom, with prefabricated buildings common in the 1950s. The curriculum focused on traditional subjects, discipline was strict and rote learning was standard. GCE O-levels, introduced in 1951, standardised exams, while higher education remained limited, with university seen as an option for the few. In 1970, approximately 14.1 per cent of the 18 to 24-year-old population in the UK attended university (Bolton 2012). By 2000, this had risen to around 41.7 per cent, reflecting a significant expansion in access to higher education over the three decades.

By the late 1950s and early 1960s, comprehensive schools started replacing the secondary modern and grammar schools. In the new system, pupils were streamed by ability within the same school rather than being placed into different schools according to academic ability as tested in the 11-plus examination. The 1972 Education Act meant that children had to stay on at school until the age of 16, which impacted younger Boomers. Meanwhile, teaching methods started to modernise, with new technologies such as projectors and even early computers. Rising aspirations and the cultural shifts of the 1960s brought fresh perspectives on creativity and equality. While the education system wasn't perfect, Baby Boomers witnessed the foundation of modern schooling and were among the first to benefit from its broader opportunities.

At work

The Baby Boomer generation entered the workforce at a time when jobs were often for life, which is in stark contrast to the more transient careers of today. In the UK, Boomers stepped into industries dominated by manufacturing, public service and emerging office-based roles. With so few going to university, apprenticeships, vocational training and steady progression were the hallmarks of their early careers. For many, there was a clear ladder to climb and job security was a given, with the accepted mantra being that if you worked hard, you could expect a long career, a pension and a gold watch at retirement.

It's fair to say that, alongside Gen X, Baby Boomers have witnessed and experienced the greatest transformation in workplace culture. They have seen shifts in equal rights, embraced greater accountability and navigated the complexities of technology and globalisation. Their journey through the workplace coincided with seismic shifts in work patterns and societal attitudes. In the UK, the 1970s brought the peak of union power, with strikes and industrial action highlighting the importance of workers' rights and collective bargaining. The era saw a divide between management holding on to traditional work methods and workers focusing on the value of solidarity to oversee a power shift.

The 1980s brought a new chapter, with Margaret Thatcher's UK government reshaping the workplace landscape. Elsewhere, the Reagan administration brought huge change in the US, while there were massive shifts in Eastern Europe. In the UK, privatisation and deregulation had a dramatic impact on traditional industries, while a culture of individualism began to emerge. British households were encouraged to buy shares in utilities with advertisements on TV. In 1986, the UK government launched the 'Tell Sid' campaign to encourage the public to purchase shares in the newly privatised British Gas. The campaign featured advertisements depicting various individuals searching for 'Sid', a representation of the average person, to inform them about the opportunity to buy shares. This initiative led to approximately 1.5 million people investing and an attitude change for many British people towards share ownership.

The effects of all this change were felt differently depending on where you were in the world and indeed within the UK. Baby Boomers adapted, many moving into the growing service and finance sectors, particularly in the south of Britain, while others further north felt the harsh impact of redundancies and deindustrialisation. According to Jim Tomlinson writing in *Contemporary British History* (2021), the appreciation of the British pound during this period made exports more expensive and imports cheaper, leading to a decline in industrial profitability and mass redundancies. In contrast, countries such as Germany and Japan saw their manufacturing sectors thrive during the same period. Both nations implemented policies that supported industrial growth, technological advancement and export-led strategies, contributing to their manufacturing booms. This divergence in industrial fortunes highlights the contrasting economic paths taken by these countries during the 1980s, which will have had a huge impact on those living through this era.

By the early 2000s, in Britain and Europe the workplace had become more globalised and tech driven, with a greater emphasis on inclusivity, equal opportunities and the importance of lifelong learning. Yet again, Baby Boomers not only adapted to these changes but often led them, championing diversity and more equitable workplaces. Their resilience and adaptability have left an indelible mark, setting the stage for the workforces that followed.

By the 2010s, when the first Boomers were due to retire, many continued the trend set by the previous generation of working past what was considered traditional retirement age. They were generally healthier than previous generations at their age and whether it was for financial reasons or just a desire for continued purpose, many kept working. According to a 2023 Pew Research Center report, in 2023, 19 per cent of the US workforce were over age 65, which is nearly double what it was 35 years ago (Fry & Braga 2023). This means the age range in the workplace is becoming greater than ever, causing its own challenges for management and teams alike.

The Covid effect

After the Silent Generation, older Baby Boomers were the next most vulnerable to the Covid-19 virus. Many faced increased isolation due to social distancing measures (depending on the country in which they lived), affecting mental health and social connections. Some of those still in the workforce opted for early retirement if they could, while others were forced to quit due to health risks or job losses. For those working through the pandemic, the shift to remote work posed challenges because of unfamiliarity with technology, although most adapted over time. Concerns about the stability of retirement savings grew, with some Boomers having to support younger family members financially, affecting their own retirement savings.

The long-term effect for this generation has been an increased focus on health and reassessment of their retirement plans and financial security. Some Boomers chose to retire earlier in what was called the 'Great Resignation', which accelerated the workforce's generational shift and has left a significant gap in experienced workers. However, some are now returning to work because they either have to or they want a renewed purpose.

Expectations

Baby Boomers entered adulthood at a time of great optimism and a fairly set trajectory for their lives. They could expect steady careers, nuclear families and financial stability. Over the decades, however, their expectations evolved, influenced by the economic recessions of the 1970s and 1980s, shifting workplace dynamics and rising living costs. The once predictable pathways to success grew less certain, and Baby Boomers had to adapt. In the UK, the rapid rise in house prices worked to Boomers' advantage, but subsequent generations have struggled to follow suit, creating a sense of generational disparity.

As they approach or move through retirement, many Boomers are redefining what this phase of life looks like. The promise of a comfortable retirement funded by pensions and savings has been undermined for some by financial crises, inflation and the rising cost of living. This may be a reason that some Boomers are delaying retirement. Entering this new stage in their lives, Boomers value purpose and connection. Many seek to contribute to their communities, whether through volunteering, mentoring or activism. Health and wellbeing are key priorities, as they aim to enjoy their later years with vitality and independence. They also seek meaningful relationships, valuing time with family and the opportunity to pass down their wisdom and stories.

Globally, and certainly in the UK, Baby Boomers now expect flexibility and options, whether that's in healthcare, leisure or work. As you would expect from people of their age, their expectations have shifted from material accumulation to personal fulfilment and legacy.

Leisure

Like everything else in their lives, Baby Boomers' approach to leisure has evolved significantly over the years, reflecting their shifting priorities as well as the way in which society has changed. In their youth, they were the generation that embraced a shifting music culture and the increasing impact of television. Leisure time was often focused on youth clubs, family outings and community activities, although they were the first generation to go on foreign holidays in great numbers as children with the rise of the package holiday in the 1960s and 1970s.

As they started families, leisure time was more restricted as they bought their homes and spent their time on gardening and DIY projects. Combined with the housebuilding boom, this was the generation who were keen to 'keep up with the Joneses'. Although the concept originated in the 1950s, it was a common phrase used in the 1960s and 1970s. It describes a competitive relationship between people in a neighbourhood or group of friends and was a popular backdrop of many sitcoms of the era, epitomised by the Margo Leadbetter character in the BBC's *The Good Life*.

As Boomers moved into middle age in the 1980s and 1990s, their leisure pursuits changed as they became empty nesters, bringing a wave of prosperity for many. They began travelling and dining out more. As well as package holidays and more affordable flights, Boomers enjoyed caravanning and holiday cottages.

Today, as they move through retirement or semi-retirement, leisure is still important, but many now focus on health and wellbeing, opting for activities such as yoga, walking groups or cycling to stay fit and connected. Travel remains a major passion, with Boomers embracing longer and more adventurous trips, including cruises, cultural tours and eco-travel. A 2024 report by the Netherlands-based CBI highlights that European Baby Boomers, including those in the UK, are a substantial and affluent demographic, often considering themselves 'ageless travellers' with a keen interest in exploring diverse destinations. Interestingly, this group is particularly conscious of sustainability, preferring tour operators that are responsible and eco-friendly, which is not necessarily the perceived view of this generation.

Looking to the future, it seems likely that Boomers will favour activities that offer flexibility, fulfilment and opportunities to connect. They are increasingly tech savvy, using apps to book experiences and connect with others. They are doing so much more than previous generations at their age by pursuing hobbies, volunteering and learning new skills well into their later years. For Boomers, leisure is not just about relaxation; it's about staying engaged, curious and purposeful.

Attitudes to money

Over the decades, Baby Boomers' attitudes to financial matters have been influenced by economic landscapes, societal changes and, as you would expect, personal milestones. They were brought up with traditional values when it came to finance and because they reached milestones such as starting a family sooner than generations today, responsibility came earlier too. Apart from limited bank overdraft availability, on the whole this generation didn't get into debt. Credit cards weren't common in the UK until the 1970s, after Barclaycard introduced the first credit card for the general public in 1966.

The economic turmoil and recessions of the 1970s and 1980s, as well as changes to the pension system in the UK, prompted a rethink of financial priorities, with a shift towards greater responsibility on individuals to manage their retirement savings. Perhaps due to their stage of life, Boomers seem to show low-risk appetites when it comes to their money. Research by savings and investments company Aegon revealed that 39 per cent of individuals over 55 had zero risk appetite and 28 per cent described their risk appetite as low (Active Financial Planners 2019).

One area where, despite fluctuations in the housing market and interest rates, Boomers have benefited greatly is in the value of their homes. This has caused friction with younger generations, although some Millennials and Gen Z are now profiting from what has been dubbed the 'Great Wealth Transfer'. An estimated £5.5 trillion is expected to pass from Boomers to younger generations in the UK over the next few decades (Phillips 2022). This will clearly impact both older and younger generations but will show an increasing divide between those who inherit wealth and those who don't.

Looking ahead, Baby Boomers are expected to continue prioritising financial security, with an emphasis on maintaining a comfortable retirement and ensuring their wealth benefits future generations. Their substantial economic influence, particularly in property ownership and accumulated assets, will play a pivotal role in shaping economic trends and wealth distribution patterns in the UK and globally.

Summing up the accepted view of the Baby Boomer generation

As this radical generation heads towards older age, they can look back at the indelible mark they have left on the world. They were the architects of cultural revolutions, technological advancements and societal transformations. In the UK, they lived through the rise of the NHS and The Beatles, and have seen the evolution of women's rights and social mobility. Their sheer numbers have given them tremendous collective power, and their attitudes have shaped an era of progress and growth.

Today, most Baby Boomers are navigating their retirement but, in many ways, have also redefined it. As the most youthful retirees in history, many remain active contributors to society, championing causes, mentoring younger generations and pursuing lifelong ambitions. However, they also face challenges, from adapting to the digital age to addressing the realities of ageing in a rapidly changing world.

Looking at their impact on younger generations, they have led the way in what it means to challenge the status quo by embracing both opportunity and responsibility. However, there may be conflict with some who see Boomers as fortunate because of their ability to accumulate a level of wealth that younger generations may not be able to. While Boomers' wealth and influence have shaped economies, many will suggest that their choices have left younger generations grappling with environmental concerns, housing crises and shifting social norms.

Again, as I will keep repeating in this book, this is an overview of the accepted take on a transformative generation and, as you will see in Section 3 when I discuss my survey results, there are probably more exceptions to the somewhat generalised Baby Boomer stereotype.

7 Generation X

Born between 1965 and 1980

Often described as the generation caught between the cultural dominance of the Baby Boomers and the digital savvy of Millennials, and sometimes referred to as the 'Middle Generation', Gen X witnessed the shift from industrial to information-based economies and a rapidly evolving cultural landscape. Just think how much the world changed during their formative years of the 1970s and 1980s, from the evolution of technology such as communications and computers to the cold war, nuclear threats and changing economies.

Who are they?

Generation X is often defined by its independence, pragmatism and adaptability. Frequently referred to as the 'latchkey kids', many grew up letting themselves in after school as both parents worked juggling jobs and family. More and more were also being brought up in single-parent households. This environment bred a sense of self-reliance during a time of rapid social and economic change. The term certainly applied to me and many of my friends whose parents both worked long hours, so as teenagers we would come home to an empty house.

The label 'Generation X' came into popular use in the early 1990s, after a short-lived stint as the 'Baby Busters'. It was Douglas Coupland's 1991 novel *Generation X: Tales for an Accelerated Culture* that cemented the name. The book followed three young adults navigating consumerism, disillusionment and a changing world, capturing the mood of a generation sceptical of traditional values and promises of progress.

An article in *Forbes* referred to Gen X as the 'forgotten generation' (Woo 2018), a label that gained traction in the 1990s, due to its position between the larger and louder Baby Boomer and Millennial cohorts. Unlike Boomers, who rode the wave of post-war prosperity, or Millennials, who came of age during the tech boom, Gen X lacked defining societal markers.

Yet their impact is undeniable. They've quietly shaped the modern world, bridging the analogue traditions of their youth with the digital innovation of today. Now in midlife, Gen X continues to sit squarely between older and younger generations, both culturally and technologically. As I explained with my Five Circles of Generational Influence model in Chapter 3, life stages will have a massive impact on a generation. In 2025, the oldest Gen Xers turned 60 and are now looking toward retirement. Some have already stepped out of full-time roles, others have become self-employed, and many are re-evaluating what they want from work, life and legacy. Meanwhile, the youngest Gen Xers are only 45, so the 15-year spread in this generation is now significant.

When it comes to preferred communication styles, the popular view is that Gen Xers prefer email and texting, and their style is usually direct and efficient – we'll see in Section 3 whether that bears out.

While Gen X inherited the Boomers' individualism, they adapted it to the sharp-edged capitalism of the 1980s, pushing boundaries for women and minorities and questioning the conventions of the workplace. They may be 'forgotten' in popular culture, but their role in shaping both society and the workforce is far from insignificant.

Notable figures

These are the people who framed the era.

- **Music:** Kurt Cobain (1967), Kylie Minogue (1968), Mariah Carey (1970), Eminem (1972), Robbie Williams (1974), Kanye West (1977).

- **Acting:** Julia Roberts (1967), Hugh Jackman (1968), Will Smith (1968), Matt Damon (1970), Christopher Nolan (1970), Leonardo DiCaprio (1974), Heath Ledger (1979).

- **Leaders:** David Cameron (1966), Justin Trudeau (1971), Emmanuel Macron (1977).

- **Business:** Michael Dell (1965), Elon Musk (1971), Larry Page (1973), Sergey Brin (1973).

- **Sport:** Steffi Graf (1969), Tiger Woods (1975), David Beckham (1975), Kobe Bryant (1978).

- **Other:** J K Rowling (1965), Damien Hirst (1965), Alexander McQueen (1969), Kate Moss (1974), Banksy (birth date unknown but it's thought to be 1970s).

First car

For Generation X, buying their first car was a mix of excitement and financial challenge. During this time, many Gen Xers faced economic uncertainty, with high interest rates, inflation and a competitive job market. For many, the option of buying a new vehicle was out of reach, so most opted for second-hand cars. These were often older models that came with the risks of wear and tear but were more affordable, especially for young people just starting their careers or finishing school. The process was often about practicality over luxury – Gen Xers valued reliability, fuel efficiency and affordability, particularly as many were just beginning to establish their financial independence. The cars they would have bought included the Ford Escort Mark 2 (1974), Volkswagen Golf Mark 1 (1974), Ford Fiesta Mark 1 (1976), Austin Mini Metro (1980), Vauxhall Nova (1983) and Peugeot 205 (1983).

Iconic coming-of-age films

The films of the time mirrored Gen X's values of independence, scepticism towards authority and a sometimes dark sense of humour, offering a cinematic escape from the pressures and challenges they faced. Big movies for Gen Xers were: *Grease* (1978), *ET* (1982), *Blade Runner* (1982), *The Breakfast Club* (1985), *The Goonies* (1985), *Back to the Future* (1985), *Top Gun* (1986), *Ferris Bueller's Day Off* (1986), *Dirty Dancing* (1987), *The Commitments* (1991) and *Trainspotting* (1996).

Young lives

Born between 1965 and 1980, this cohort grew up in a different world from their predecessors, witnessing the economic upheaval of the 1970s, the deregulation and privatisation of the 1980s. This age group were children and adolescents when the threat of nuclear war seemed a frightening possibility, marked by a sharp increase in hostility between the United States and the Soviet Union. I remember the real fear instilled by the 'Protect and Survive' public information campaign and *Threads*, a harrowing drama depicting the aftermath of a nuclear attack in Sheffield. The late 80s saw 'Glasnost' in the then Soviet Union, the fall of the Berlin Wall in 1989, followed by the dawn of the digital era in the 1990s. It was a remarkable time to live through. Unlike the Boomers, who saw the optimism and relative stability of the 1950s and 1960s, many Gen Xers were growing up in dual-income households with rising divorce rates and an emphasis on self-reliance. More choice on TV and the first video games emerged for this generation, leading to a new way of being entertained in between riding their bikes without helmets and riding on go-karts without any brakes. This was the beginning of what would be seen as a risk-taking generation.

Education

For many, school in the UK was changing from the grammar school system to comprehensive education, and older Gen Xers were learning about decimalisation in the early 1970s from Baby

Boomer teachers who weren't too sure about it themselves. The trend of youngsters staying in education had started to increase in the 1970s and between 1980–81 and 1993–94 this grew further. According to statistics in the House of Commons Library staying-on rates for 16-year-olds increased from 42 per cent to 74 per cent, while the rate for 17-year-olds went from 27 per cent to 58 per cent. This compares to 76 per cent of 17-year-olds in full-time education in 2011 (Bolton 2012).

At work

In Britain, Gen X came of age during a period of huge change, with the decline of traditional industries such as steelmaking, mining and shipbuilding, and the growth of the service sectors such as banking, insurance and hospitality. The impact of this cultural shift very much depended on which part of the country you were in at the time with the extremes of the yuppies in London to the mining and steelmaking communities in the north. These events fostered a pragmatic and adaptable mindset out of need rather than choice.

Entering adulthood during economic instability, Gen X faced fewer guarantees of stable employment and saw the erosion of long-term corporate loyalty. This may have led to being labelled the 'Slacker Generation'. Coupland's *Generation X* (1991) explored the lives of disillusioned, directionless young adults, further cementing the 'slacker' stereotype. Gen Xers grew up with a more sceptical and less idealistic view of work. However, many in Gen X pushed back against this label, arguing that their perceived 'slacker' attitude was a response to the lack of opportunities, rather than laziness or a shortage of ambition.

Despite the challenges, many Gen Xers earned a reputation for resilience, adaptability and independence. Their formative experiences, from latchkey childhoods to navigating uncertain job markets prepared them to adapt in a world of constant change.

Gen Xers are the bridge between retiring Boomers and younger Millennials and Gen Z, although with many now in their fifties, the eldest are contemplating retirement themselves. They are balancing watching out for their Gen Z (or young

Millennial) children while looking after their Silent Generation parents. Unlike the Boomers, who often found steady jobs in structured workplaces, Gen X has learned to thrive in a more flexible, fast-paced environment.

They were there before the internet took over and adapted seamlessly when it did, which makes them uniquely positioned to navigate both old-school processes and new technologies. After all, they started their careers well before email and smartphones. This unique perspective makes them problem solvers who aren't easily fazed by change. Having grown up in a time when nothing was guaranteed, they tend to be flexible, pragmatic and self-sufficient.

The Covid effect

Balancing remote work with caregiving responsibilities for both children and elderly parents was the major challenge facing Generation X during the pandemic. They were pivotal in adapting to new technologies and processes in the workplace, often acting as leaders and problem solvers. A 2021 study that examined how different generations responded to job insecurity during the pandemic suggested that as well as the direct health impact, Gen X suffered from increased stress and burnout as a result of juggling multiple roles, and this had a direct impact on their mental health and wellbeing (Mahmoud et al 2021). They also had concerns about the health of vulnerable, ageing parents with the risk of virus exposure, so were very mindful of shielding. With a renewed emphasis on achieving a healthier work–life balance, older Gen Xers have looked at ways to retire early, work part time or even change to a less stressful career.

Expectations

Like every generation before them, as Gen X move through midlife, their expectations have shifted. With many in their late forties to mid-fifties, they're at a stage where they want stability but also flexibility. Having grown up in a world that taught them to expect change and adapt, they're not looking for rigid, one-size-fits-all solutions – whether it's in the workplace, in their personal lives or from society at large. They've worked hard, they've adapted countless times, and now they expect some payoff for that effort.

Financial security is another major expectation. After enduring multiple economic crises – from the recessions of the 1980s and early 1990s to the financial crash of 2008 – Gen X is keenly aware of the need to prepare for retirement. Unlike generations before them, they don't necessarily expect to fully retire in the traditional sense. Many see themselves continuing to work in some capacity, whether by consulting, freelancing or pursuing passion projects.

On a personal level, they prioritise wellbeing and meaningful experiences. Having grown up in an era of materialism but matured in a world that increasingly values purpose, Gen X is more interested in quality of life. They've seen the downside of burnout culture and are now looking for a more sustainable approach to life, whether that means travelling more, spending time with family or simply finding joy in everyday moments.

Leisure

Leisure time for Gen X has evolved just as much as their work lives. When they were younger, free time for this generation was exactly that. They had lots of freedom, from watching Saturday morning cartoons to making mixtapes or heading out with friends on their bikes – if it was in the UK, the chances are it would have been a Chopper. While the amount of content for young people was growing, it wasn't on demand and socialising was normally face to face, with phone calls still costly in the 1970s. They embraced pop culture through music TV shows like *Top of the Pops*, rented VHS tapes from the video store, and found their tribe in everything from punk rock gigs to early gaming communities.

As they moved into adulthood, leisure started to shift. In their twenties and thirties, it was about concerts, pubs and clubbing – experiences that were as much about bonding with friends as about having fun. Many Gen Xers travelled extensively, often backpacking through Europe or South-East Asia, drawn by a desire to explore and experience the world first hand. They didn't have social media to document every moment, but that didn't stop them from making memories. This generation still started families at a relatively young age compared to today and were keen to get on the property ladder. Along with the economic uncertainty, this led to more nights in, looking after children and decorating.

Now, in midlife, leisure looks a little different. It's less about late nights out and more about finding balance and recharging. For many, that means spending quality time with family, whether through weekend hikes, game nights or simply catching up over dinner. Fitness and wellness have also become key priorities. From yoga classes to mindfulness apps, Gen X has embraced the idea that leisure can be about self-care, not just entertainment.

Technology has played a huge role in reshaping their downtime. Streaming services have replaced video rentals, podcasts have taken over from radio shows, and online gaming has become a way to unwind. Yet, despite all the digital options, many Gen Xers still appreciate the analogue joys of a good book or a vinyl record. They've learned to blend old-school hobbies with modern conveniences, finding a balance that suits their lifestyle.

At this stage in life, for Gen X leisure is about more than just passing the time; it's about doing things that matter. Whether that's learning a new skill, volunteering or simply taking time to relax, Gen X approaches leisure with the same pragmatic, no-nonsense attitude that has defined them all along. They've moved from mixtapes to mindfulness, but the spirit remains the same: find what you love and make time for it.

Attitudes to money

Gen X's attitude to money has been shaped by a mix of hard lessons and evolving priorities. Having grown up in the shadow of economic recessions and witnessing first hand the financial struggles of their parents, they developed a cautious, pragmatic approach to finances early on. This led to Gen X never fully buying into the promise of guaranteed prosperity, so they learned to save, plan and prepare for the unexpected. This was also the first generation who would have access to credit cards as they left school and entered the workplace.

In Britain, where the 1980s were marked by significant economic upheaval, many Gen Xers saw their communities impacted by the decline of manufacturing and the rise of service industries. The Thatcher era, with its emphasis on individual responsibility and home ownership, left a lasting impression. For many, getting on the property ladder became a key financial goal, and many embraced DIY and home renovation. Their parents were the make-do-and-mend generation, so many were able to share skills with their offspring. This was also the era of housing booms and busts as well as big fluctuations in interest rates, which reached a peak of 17 per cent in 1979 and 15 per cent in the late 1980s and early 1990s (Bank of England 2025). All this uncertainty had a big impact on their financial confidence, causing them to continually adjust their plans.

As they've grown older, their focus has shifted from simply building wealth to ensuring long-term financial security. They're keenly aware of the need to prepare for retirement, having seen pension schemes change and state support become less certain. In the UK, the decline of final salary pensions has meant that Gen Xers have had to take more responsibility for their own retirement savings. Many have turned to personal pensions, ISAs and property as ways to secure their financial future.

Despite their cautious approach, they're not afraid to spend money on what matters. Experiences, whether it's travel, dining or hobbies, take priority over material possessions. Gen X values getting good value for their money but aren't afraid to splurge on meaningful moments. They are now focusing on enjoying life while being prepared for whatever comes next. Their attitude to money reflects their overall outlook: practical, self-reliant and always ready to adapt – despite some being labelled as the 'Slacker Generation' in their twenties.

Summing up the accepted view of Gen X

Gen Xers have navigated an ever-changing world with a mix of realism, resilience and resourcefulness. From growing up as latchkey kids to becoming digital pioneers, they've had to adapt to shifting cultural, economic and technological landscapes and on the whole their pragmatic approach has meant they've done it without much fanfare.

What defines them now, in midlife, is a desire for balance between work and life, saving and spending, responsibility and enjoyment. They've learned to prioritise what matters most, whether that's family, wellbeing or financial security. They're not a generation looking for the spotlight; instead, they're focused on living a life that feels meaningful on their own terms.

As they move into the next phase of life, Gen Xers will continue to shape the world around them in subtle but significant ways. They're not about grand declarations or sweeping trends; they're about showing up, doing the work and adapting to whatever comes next. And perhaps that's what makes them so influential today, because while they may not always be seen, they're always making an impact.

8 Millennials (Gen Y)

Born between 1981 and 1996

By the early 2000s, it was time to name the next generation. The easy solution was Generation Y, simply because Y comes after X. However, just like 'Baby Busters' was replaced by Gen X, the term Gen Y didn't stick. Instead, Neil Howe and William Strauss's *Millennials Rising* (2009) named the generation after the new era in which they came of age, and Millennials is the label that has endured.

Who are they?

Often characterised as tech savvy, collaborative and values driven, this generation has been the focus of countless debates and headlines. As the children of Baby Boomers, Millennials came of age during the digital revolution, economic upheavals and a shift towards more socially conscious thinking.

While Generation X transitioned from an analogue to a digital world, Millennials lived through the internet's full emergence. They're not quite digital natives as they learned the technology as it appeared – but they were the first to make social media part of daily life. That exposure has profoundly shaped how they communicate, work and engage with the world.

Generally, they favour fast, digital communication and have a strong preference for collaboration – a word that comes up often when describing this group. As Paul Gentile, senior product marketing director at GoTo, noted in a 2019 blog post, Millennials are 'driving a new collaborative work style', influencing workplace dynamics with their appetite for teamwork and open communication.

Born into a rapidly globalising world, Millennials saw personal computers, mobile phones and eventually the internet become household staples. They witnessed major global events – 9/11, the 2008 financial crisis – alongside the rise of platforms such as Facebook and Instagram. In the UK, this was also a time of increased educational opportunity, with government measures extending time spent in education and growing awareness around environmental and social issues in the 1990s and early 2000s.

Although often described as optimistic, this is a generation weighed down by student debt, rising living costs and a more precarious job market than their predecessors. Shaped by a culture of self-expression and individualism, they've been both criticised and celebrated. Joel Stein, in his 2013 *Time* magazine article on 'The me me me generation', described Millennials as having a 'self-focused upbringing' that contributed to perceptions of narcissism and entitlement – highlighting behaviours such as emailing CEOs directly and avoiding less stimulating projects.

Yet alongside this individualism is a strong desire for connection. Millennials are also known for seeking regular feedback, thriving in team settings and prioritising experiences over possessions. They're a generation defined as much by their values as by their screens – and how they choose to use both.

Notable figures

These are the people who have framed the era.

- **Music:** Justin Timberlake (1981), Beyoncé (1981), Amy Winehouse (1983), Drake (1986), Rihanna (1988), Taylor Swift (1989), Ed Sheeran (1991), Miley Cyrus (1992), Ariana Grande (1993), Justin Bieber (1994), Harry Styles (1994).

- ⚟ **Acting:** Chris Hemsworth (1983), Scarlett Johansen (1984), Emma Watson (1990).

- ⚟ **Leaders:** Jacinda Ardern (1980), Prince William (1982), Kim Jong-un (1984).

- ⚟ **Business:** Mark Zuckerberg (1984), Melanie Perkins (1987), Fraser Doherty (1988), Patrick Collinson (1988), Whitney Wolfe Herd (1989), Ritesh Agarwa (1993).

- ⚟ **Sport:** Serena Williams (1981), Lewis Hamilton (1985), Cristiano Ronaldo (1985), Jessica Ennis-Hill (1986), Usain Bolt (1986), Andy Murray (1987), Novak Đjoković (1987), Hannah Cockroft (1992), Raheem Sterling (1994).

- ⚟ **Other:** Nadiya Hussain (chef, 1984), Harley Weir (photographer, 1988), Avicii (DJ, 1989), Kendall Jenner (model, 1995).

First car

Like the generations before them, for Millennials in the UK buying their first car was often a significant financial milestone marked by a mix of excitement and caution. However, many Millennials faced challenges with affordability due to the rising cost of living, insurance and, for some, relatively low starting salaries. As a result, most opted for second-hand cars rather than new ones, often looking for older, more affordable models that were still reliable but less expensive. Millennials were more cautious and practical in their choices compared with previous generations, focusing on fuel efficiency and low insurance costs. In the UK, passing the driving test was more challenging for Millennials compared to previous generations, with tougher practical tests and a more rigorous theory exam, making it harder for many young people to obtain their driving licence. This shift reflected increased concerns about road safety and a desire to ensure that new drivers were better prepared for the challenges of modern driving. Their first cars were typically the Vauxhall Corsa (1993), Ford Fiesta Mark 4 (1995), Renault Clio Mark 2 (1998), Volkswagen Polo Mark 3 (1994), Toyota Yaris (1999) and Fiat Punto Mark 2 (1999).

Iconic coming-of-age films

These films represent the different stages of Millennial growth – from childhood and adolescence to young adulthood. They cover a wide range of experiences, from high school drama and friendship to tackling serious life challenges, and they each left a lasting impact on the Millennial generation. As well as the cinema, this generation were brought up on DVDs, with many families acquiring a film library on DVD or Blu-ray. A growing number of satellite TV channels also became available in the 1990s and early 2000s as the UK caught up with other countries – especially the US. The movies Millennials will possibly have watched numerous times include: *Jurassic Park* (1993), *The Lion King* (1994), *Four Weddings and a Funeral* (1994), *Titanic* (1998), *10 Things I Hate About You* (1999), *American Pie* (1999), *Billy Elliot* (2000), the *Harry Potter* series (2001–11), *Mean Girls* (2004), *The Holiday* (2006) and *This Is England* (2006).

Young lives

As I have mentioned before, to understand how a generation thinks, it's important to consider who their parents are, and for Millennials they were mostly Baby Boomers. Some people, including me, believe that Baby Boomer parenting styles contributed to a more child-centred society and perceptions of entitlement among Millennials. In *Kid Power, Inequalities and Intergenerational Relations* (2021), Rübner Jørgensen and Wyness argue that late 20th-century parenting marked a pivotal shift towards prioritising children's needs and voices, driven by social, political and economic changes. This shift coincided with Baby Boomers becoming parents who, unlike their more distant and disciplinarian predecessors, sought to be actively engaged in their children's upbringing. This more attentive parenting approach, including 'helicopter parenting' practices, aimed to prepare children for success by offering constant support and removing potential obstacles. This increased parental involvement fostered a child-centred environment, where children were seen as active participants within the family unit rather than passive dependents.

Having said that, it's important to understand that

generational dynamics are influenced by a complex interplay of cultural, economic and institutional factors. While Millennials may have benefited from greater attention and opportunities, they also face societal expectations and challenges that complicate the narrative of entitlement and privilege often associated with them. Their formative years were marked by rapid technological changes, from dial-up internet and basic mobile phones to broadband and smartphones. Social media became a defining part of their lives, changing how they interacted with friends, consumed news and built their identities. It was a time of relative peace but also increasing economic instability. In the UK, many Millennials remember Tony Blair's government, the rise of Cool Britannia and an era of optimism around globalisation.

Education

Education played a crucial role in shaping Millennials. In the UK in 1999, then prime minister Tony Blair announced a target for 50 per cent of young adults to enter higher education in the UK, which was attained by 2019 (Gov.uk 2022). This had a far-reaching impact on Millennials in relation to careers and the workplace. It was also a marked difference compared with the much lower higher education rates for Generation X, which in 1988 stood at just over 15 per cent (Hansard 1989).

The move also led to the Higher Education Act 2004, which introduced measures such as variable tuition fees to provide universities with additional funding. As a result, many Millennials left university burdened by significant student debt. The promise of a graduate premium in terms of better jobs and higher wages for those with degrees didn't always materialise, particularly after the 2008 financial crash. As a result, many Millennials have struggled with underemployment and job insecurity, which has influenced their views on work and money.

In the late 1980s, UK schools began shifting their approach to sports, emphasising participation over competition. The aim was to make sports more inclusive, by encouraging all students to engage regardless of skill level. The introduction of participation trophies became a symbol of this movement, intended to boost children's confidence and foster a sense of belonging. However, this well-intentioned approach sparked a big debate. Critics argued that rewarding mere participation could dilute the value of genuine achievement and fail to teach children resilience and the realities of competition. Proponents, on the other hand, believed that such recognition can motivate continued involvement in sports and promote teamwork.

The long-term impact on the generation schooled during this era is mixed. A 2021 article from *Physical & Health Education America*, for example, suggested that while participation trophies can motivate children to engage in sports by recognising their involvement, potentially fostering continued interest and attendance, critics argue that awarding trophies for mere participation might diminish a child's intrinsic motivation to improve and achieve, potentially leading to decreased resilience and an inability to handle failure or criticism (Roos & Strand 2021). While in *Psychology Today* (2023), Candida Fink suggests such trophies celebrate children's participation, regardless of success or failure, and protect their emotional health. Many schools today strive to balance inclusivity and healthy competition.

In 2008, the age at which youngsters could leave school was raised again to 18 in the Education and Skills Act, which meant youngsters were older as they entered the workplace.

At work

Millennials joined the workforce at a turbulent time, with the 2008 global financial crisis striking just as many were beginning their careers. This upheaval created a tougher job market with fewer stable, long-term roles. Unlike Boomers and Gen X, who often remained in one position for years, Millennials earned a reputation for job hopping. This was less about disloyalty and more out of necessity, driven by the need to adapt to rapidly changing circumstances.

Rather than sticking to the traditional career ladder, Millennials looked for purpose-driven roles, flexibility and a better work–life balance. They became early adopters of freelancing, entrepreneurship and side hustles, not just as a means to stay afloat, but as a way to shape their own career paths. This generation's entry into the workplace didn't just prompt opinions; it sparked debate. Every emerging generation faces scrutiny, but Millennials' arrival brought sharper focus and greater curiosity about generational differences.

This interest was captured perfectly in Simon Sinek's 2016 talk 'Millennials in the workplace', which has since had more than 13 million views. It was a pivotal moment that first piqued my fascination with generational dynamics. In the video, Sinek explores how Millennials' approach to work differs from that of earlier generations, particularly in their demand for change. They championed remote work, mental health awareness and initiatives promoting diversity and inclusion. In the UK, their influence extended to reshaping the labour market, driving the growth of the gig economy and embracing unconventional career paths.

Being an entrepreneur also changed radically for this generation. Previously, entrepreneurs harnessed the tools available to them to create groundbreaking ventures, but for Millennials, technology has proven to be the game changer. Unlike previous generations, for whom starting a business often required significant capital or infrastructure, Millennials leveraged digital tools to disrupt industries and connect with global audiences.

Take Fraser Doherty, a Scottish entrepreneur who turned his grandmother's jam recipes into an international brand by the age of 14. Initially selling door to door and at farmers' markets, Doherty's innovative spirit quickly scaled when he began leveraging online platforms to expand his customer base. By the time he was approached by the high-end UK supermarket Waitrose, his SuperJam products had already built a reputation for their quality and authenticity. A few years later, he tapped into the power of ecommerce and international shopping networks, selling £1 million worth of merchandise in a single hour in South Korea. Doherty's journey exemplifies how Millennials blend traditional craftsmanship with the global reach of technology.

Similarly, John and Patrick Collison, the Irish brothers behind Stripe, demonstrate the technological prowess that defines Millennial entrepreneurship. From their teenage years, they identified a gap in the market, which was to create an easy way for businesses to process online payments. By building Stripe, they created a seamless solution that revolutionised financial transactions for companies worldwide. Their story highlights how coding and technological innovation can transform industries, enabling businesses of all sizes to thrive in a digital economy.

The internet, coding skills and global connectivity have allowed Millennial entrepreneurs to dream bigger, launch faster and make a more significant mark at younger ages than ever before. Combining digital tech advancement and entrepreneurial spirit may have begun with Millennials, but what they have achieved is a mere glimpse into the limitless potential that future generations will continue to build upon.

Millennials employed by others were also looking to change the old ways of working. They wanted something new, something better and in doing so have reshaped the workplace for everyone who came after them. As the Millennials take up more senior roles in organisations, they are now managing a whole new generation who have continued the trajectory of change.

The Covid effect

Millennials faced significant career disruptions during the pandemic, with job losses and furloughs affecting financial stability and many were already burdened by student debt. Major life milestones such as buying homes, getting married or having children were delayed due to financial uncertainties and the physical ability to move or book wedding venues. However, they also adapted quickly. Having grown up in a digital world, they were well equipped to handle the shift to remote work and virtual socialising. When they could move house, many chose to take advantage of remote work and relocated to more affordable areas, often to suburbs and more rural locations. Millennials reported high levels of anxiety and depression, exacerbated by isolation and financial stress, as reported by researchers (Mahmoud et al 2021). Many sought mental health resources during the pandemic and, looking forward, there seems to be a strong focus on mental health support for this generation as well as job security and workplace flexibility. The pandemic also accelerated their push for flexible working arrangements, greater work–life balance and mental health awareness in the workplace.

Expectations

Millennials have high expectations for themselves as well as the world around them. They value authenticity, transparency and social responsibility. They expect brands to take a stand on social issues, employers to prioritise wellbeing and governments to address climate change and inequality.

Financially, they're focused on stability, and many have delayed traditional milestones due to economic pressures. Instead, they prioritise saving, investing and finding ways to enjoy life despite financial constraints. With most Millennials now in their thirties, they continue to value the collaboration and fairness that have always been a key part of their life's expectations.

Leisure

This was the first generation to grow up with gaming, with the Nintendo Game Boy going on sale in 1989, followed by the first Sony PlayStation in 1995. On TV, they were watching an even greater variety of child-centric programming and, given the affordability of TV sets, they were more often watching programmes in their bedrooms and not with the rest of the family. This was when they weren't busy attending activities organised by their Boomer parents. As they grew up, leisure was about experiences for Millennials. Unlike the nesting generations before them, who may have focused on accumulating possessions, Millennials have always valued making memories. For some, this may be because of the frustration of not being able to afford a home of their own. They enjoy travel, dining out, attending events and trying new experiences. Technology plays a central role in their leisure time. Streaming services, social media and gaming are popular pastimes. Fitness and wellness have also become major trends, with many Millennials investing in gym memberships, yoga classes and wellness retreats.

Attitudes to money

Millennials have a complicated relationship with money. On one hand, they're known for their spending on experiences and self-care. On the other, they're often criticised for not saving enough. The reality is that many Millennials face financial pressures that previous generations didn't, from proportionally higher housing costs to student loan repayments. Student loans started in the UK in 1990 and in 1998 the Teaching and Higher Education Act introduced tuition fees. These controversially replaced maintenance grants with income-contingent loans. According to UK government figures, by 2023 average student debt in the UK had reached a massive £45,600, which has placed a huge burden on Millennials and the generations that have followed (Bolton 2024). Additionally, this cohort witnessed the financial turbulence of the late Noughties, so they tend to be financially more risk averse and despite the opportunity to get into debt they are more reluctant compared with generations before them.

In Britain, rising property prices have made home ownership a distant dream for many. While some have managed to get on the property ladder with help from schemes like Help to Buy, or from the Bank of Mum and Dad, many others continue to rent well into their thirties.

Despite these challenges, Millennials are financially savvy. They are more likely to invest in stocks, cryptocurrency and peer-to-peer lending platforms than previous generations. They prioritise financial education and are keen on finding new ways to build wealth.

Summing up the accepted view of Millennials (Gen Y)

This is a pivotal generation that led the way when it came to their upbringing, with the world becoming more child focused. Millennials have also faced their fair share of challenges, from economic downturns to a rapidly changing world. While often misunderstood, they've embraced change, pushed for progress and found ways to thrive in uncertain times.

What defines them is their adaptability, their focus on

experiences and their desire to create a better world through collaboration and social awareness. Millennials may feel they have not had it easy, but as they move into midlife they've learned to persevere, and that perseverance is what makes them truly unique.

9 Generation Z
Born between 1997 and 2011

Gen Z is probably the most talked about generation today, as other generations all strive to understand them. The term 'Generation Z' logically followed Generation X and Generation Y (Millennials), so it emerged as a placeholder name in demographic and marketing discussions. *Generation Z: A Century in the Making* (2018) by Corey Seemiller and Meghan Grace later helped define the characteristics of the group more formally.

Who are they?

Gen Z, sometimes called Zoomers, are the first true digital natives. Unlike Millennials, who witnessed the rise of the internet, Gen Z were born into a world of smartphones, tablets, high-speed internet and social media. They've never known life without being constantly connected – and that has shaped how they think, communicate and engage with the world.

This generation is known for its pragmatism, independence and strong sense of social justice. While Millennials are often seen as idealistic, Gen Z tends to be more realistic – and more willing to challenge those in power, including older generations.

Growing up amid economic uncertainty, the climate crisis and global instability, they've developed a sharp awareness of the challenges facing their future.

When it comes to labels, as opposed to Millennials, Generation Z appears more comfortable with their generational identity. A 2023 study conducted by Vox Media in partnership with Horowitz Research found that Gen Zers not only accept and embrace their own differences but also those of others, reflecting their position as the most diverse generation in terms of race, ethnicity and gender (Goorin & Baumgarten 2023).

Technology is at the core of their identity. They're digital multitaskers who glide between platforms, devices and apps – and for them, there's no clear divide between online and offline life. The digital world is simply part of their reality. This behaviour isn't necessarily a lack of focus, but a reflection of the environment they've grown up in.

In her book *Attention Span* (2023), Dr Gloria Mark points to her research, which began in 2004, and showed that people spent about two and a half minutes on a screen before shifting attention. By 2012, that dropped to 75 seconds. Now, it's just 47 seconds. As she notes, it's hard to say whether this shift caused changes in media, or the other way around – but the shift is real. I think there is a difference though between attention span and focus.

As neuroscientist Dr Lynda Shaw explained on my *Generationally Speaking* podcast: 'Older generations moaning about attention spans? That's ancient – Aristotle did it too.' On the idea that attention spans are shrinking, she isn't convinced, saying: 'What we're doing is switching our attention from one thing to another.'

It's a behaviour that older generations are adopting too in a world of endless streaming, scrolling and swiping. The ability to switch focus is actually a finely tuned filter – a practical response to an environment overflowing with content. As I've observed, the masters of this switching ability are indeed Gen Zers. If something doesn't engage them, they move on – not out of impatience, but because they can.

Away from screens, Gen Zers are passionate about diversity, inclusivity and authenticity. They value equality and representation, and they expect these principles to be lived out, not just talked about. They're also highly entrepreneurial – perhaps something they've inherited from their Gen X parents. While some bought and sold on eBay, others have been watching influencers and content creators turn their passions into profitable careers, and they're eager to do the same. By 2025 the older half of Gen Zers had entered the workplace and many value self-employment, side hustles and creative pursuits over traditional corporate roles. Take 23-year-old Henry Farr, for example – a guest on my *Generationally Speaking* podcast. While younger Gen Zers are still on the school bus each morning, Henry is running his own food business, cooking and serving hot meals at festivals and events.

This generation is redefining success. They're not in a rush to settle down, with many delaying marriage, children and home ownership. A 2022 UK survey by Relate found that 83 per cent of Gen Z are continuing the trend set by Millennials: pushing back traditional milestones in favour of personal experiences. This isn't just about values – financial pressures play a big part. With soaring living costs and housing prices, many Gen Zers simply can't afford the aspirations their Gen X parents achieved at the same age.

And yet, Gen Zers are known for embracing the moment. A recent study found that 81 per cent of them agree with the statement 'I try to have as much fun now and let the future look after itself' (Jolly 2024). It's a modern take on *carpe diem* – a mindset that values joy, creativity and personal growth in a world where certainty is hard to come by.

So while some label Gen Zers as distracted or overly cautious about tradition, I see a generation adapting smartly to a fast-changing world. They're redefining what it means to thrive – not by ticking boxes, but by designing a life that's meaningful, flexible and true to their values.

Notable figures

This generation is gaining fame in different ways from older generations, with YouTubers and social media stars high on the celebrity listings. With the rise of global interconnectivity, these influencers are also more internationally recognised than ever before. Although Gen Zers are still making their mark on the world, already some are emerging as those framing their era.

- ⚝ **Music:** Zara Larsson (1997), Shawn Mendes (1998), Billie Eilish (2001).

- ⚝ **Acting:** Jaden Smith (1998), Amandla Stenberg (1998), Millie Bobby Brown (2004).

- ⚝ **Sport:** Naomi Osaka (1997), Kylian Mbappé (1998), Emma Raducanu (2002).

- ⚝ **Other:** Malala Yousafzai (1997), Kylie Jenner (1997), Greta Thunberg (2003).

First car

With rising living costs and a competitive job market, many Gen Zers have found it difficult to afford a new car, so like previous generations they have typically opted for second-hand vehicles. Popular choices were small, economical cars, which were more affordable both in terms of price and insurance costs. For many in Gen Z, getting a car is still seen as a symbol of independence, but there has also been a noticeable shift in attitudes, with some preferring to rely on public transport or ridesharing services rather than owning a vehicle. The financial burden of car ownership is a consideration, with many opting for financing options or leasing rather than outright purchases. In the UK, the driving test had become more rigorous in recent years, and there was a big backlog of driving test availability during and following the pandemic. This, combined with higher insurance premiums for young drivers, made obtaining a licence and owning a car a bigger financial hurdle. For those fortunate enough to be able to buy a car, they probably chose the Toyota Aygo (2005), Vauxhall Corsa D (2006), Ford Fiesta Mark 7 (2008), Volkswagen Polo (fifth generation 2009), or Hyundai i10 (2013).

Iconic coming-of-age films

These films capture key themes of growing up, self-discovery, friendship, family and navigating complex emotions, especially in a more complex and digital world. British-born Gen Zers likely have a strong connection to these films, as many reflect their unique cultural experiences, humour and sense of identity, while also dealing with universal themes that resonate across generations. For the first time many of these films will have been watched at home on demand as well as in the cinema. Here are just some of the films that made a big impression on Gen Z: the *Harry Potter* series (2001–11), *Shaun of the Dead* (2004), *The Hunger Games* (2012), *Frozen* (2013), *Guardians of the Galaxy* (2014) and *Jumanji: Welcome to the Jungle* (2017).

Young lives

Growing up at the beginning of a new century, Gen Zers were exposed to a world of constant change and upheaval. In Britain, they witnessed the aftermath of the 2008 financial crisis, rising concerns about climate change and the Brexit debate. Many have grown up with a heightened sense of anxiety about the future, whether it's due to economic uncertainty, environmental issues or political divisions. Their connectivity has heightened their awareness of such issues from a much younger age than previous generations.

Their childhoods were shaped by rapid technological advancements. From an early age, they had access to smartphones, tablets and high-speed internet. Younger Gen Zers were approaching their teens when Snapchat (originally called Picaboo) first appeared as an app on smartphones targeting a younger audience. Along with Instagram and TikTok, these social media platforms have played a central role in their lives, influencing how they communicate, form relationships and consume information.

Peer pressure has become a major factor. Although such pressure has always existed, it has manifested itself in different ways over the generations. I recall that at the age of 15, that if I hadn't watched *Not the Nine O'Clock News* (a British satirical news programme broadcast from 1979–1982) on a Monday night, there was no point in me joining a conversation on Tuesday, because that was the main topic. For young Gen Zers it's the same, but instead they're sharing videos on TikTok or Instagram.

Education

For Gen Z, education has been heavily influenced by technology. In the UK, they've grown up with smartboards in classrooms, online learning resources and, more recently, virtual learning during the Covid-19 pandemic. They're used to instant access to information and have a preference for interactive, hands-on learning.

In my work in schools over the past ten years, I have seen the use of phones evolve from seeing them in use by students during breaks to there now being a strict ban in most of the schools where I've delivered workshops. In fact, I recently went into a school where the mobile signal had been jammed, so even the most determined youngster couldn't use their phone in a quiet corner.

Although schools have changed enormously, with far more interaction with students than before, many feel the traditional educational system hasn't always kept up with their needs. Concerns have been raised about the lack of emphasis on life skills such as financial literacy, digital skills and mental health education within the current curriculum. The curriculum is critiqued for not adequately preparing students for real-world challenges, particularly in areas such as financial literacy and technological proficiency (Scott 2024). Gen Zers place a high value on education but are also sceptical of its traditional formats. They're more likely to seek out alternative learning paths, such as online courses, bootcamps and self-directed learning, especially when it comes to gaining skills that are directly relevant to their careers.

When it comes to higher education, Gen Zers are ambitious and more than ever want to go to university. As of the 2022–23 academic year, there were approximately 2.9 million students enrolled in higher education institutions across the UK, marking a 2.77 per cent increase from the previous year, although some of these students were from overseas (HESA 2024). A significant portion of these students are opting to extend their studies beyond undergraduate programs. In 2022–23, there were 883,635 postgraduate students, with 619,795 enrolled in taught master's programmes, according to the same report.

However, the financial implications of higher education are a pressing concern. The average student loan debt in the UK has been on the rise, leading many Gen Z students to reassess the return on investment of their degrees. Research from the Centre for Global Higher Education (De Gayardon et al 2018) has shown that student loan debt negatively impacts graduates' decisions regarding career paths, home ownership and family planning. While Generation Zers in the UK remain committed to higher education, they are acutely aware of the financial burdens it entails, so in response to these challenges, apprenticeships have gained popularity. According to apprenticeship provider Starting Point, there was a 2.5 per cent increase in apprenticeships taken up in 2023 compared to the previous year (Ricardo 2024). For many it's an attractive alternative, offering practical experience and a salary, often with lower or no student debt.

At work

Gen Zers do have a thirst for knowledge, but older generations sometimes misunderstand their apparent lack of interest in finding answers to questions by asking older and more experienced people. Instead they come from an era where the natural place to search for a solution is on the internet or by watching a YouTube video. I remember asking my father about basic car maintenance when I bought my Mark 1 Ford Escort at the age of 19. Today I'd be going straight to YouTube.

Gen Zers are entering the workforce with a different set of expectations compared to previous generations. They want meaningful work, flexibility and opportunities for growth. Unlike Millennials, who were often willing to work long hours to prove themselves, Gen Z values work–life balance from the start.

According to the ADP Research Institute's *People at Work 2023: A Global Workforce View*, Gen Z workers are among the most insecure regarding their jobs, with 31 per cent expressing job insecurity, especially in the wake of economic disruptions caused by Brexit and the pandemic (Richardson & Antonello

2023). They're also vocal about the importance of mental health support in the workplace.

This is a very entrepreneurial generation – perhaps a chip off the block of their Gen X parents. Side hustles, freelance work and gig economy jobs are common. Generation Z has certainly emerged as a dynamic force when it comes to young entrepreneurs. A report in the *Times* (Ackerman 2024) reported that analysis of 2023 Office for National Statistics (ONS) figures revealed that the number of Gen Z company directors leapt by 42 per cent in 2023 to nearly 250,000. Unlike their Millennial predecessors, Gen Z have been immersed in a fully digital world from birth, making their integration of technology into business more seamless than any other generation to date.

In 2015, at just 17 years old, Akshay Ruparelia from north-east London identified a profitable opportunity within the property market, founding his first business Doorsteps, an innovative online estate agency that sold more than £1 billion worth of houses in just three years. Ben Towers is the same age as Akshay and started his digital marketing agency, Towers Design, at just 11 years old. By 23, he had co-founded Tahora, a workplace community-building app, and Richard Branson has called Towers 'one of the UK's most exciting entrepreneurs'.

Gen Zers prioritise flexibility, social impact and authenticity. They are more likely to start businesses that align with personal values and societal issues, reflecting a shift from the profit-centric models of previous generations. Gen Z entrepreneurs often begin their ventures as side hustles, balancing them alongside education or other employment. This approach allows them to test ideas in the market with minimal risk, a strategy that has been facilitated by the accessibility of online platforms and resources.

As this generation continues to mature, their influence on the business world is expected to grow, bringing fresh perspectives and innovative solutions to the forefront of the global economy. When it comes to their work life, Gen Zers want to be in control and aren't afraid to switch jobs, careers or businesses if their expectations aren't met.

The Covid effect

The youngest of Gen Z were just eight years old when the pandemic hit and they experienced significant disruptions in education, with remote learning affecting their academic progress and social development. Exams at almost every level in the UK were interrupted and for the older Gen Zers at university, remote lectures became the norm. You can't underestimate the impact of students missing out on the normal university experience and how this affected their first years away from home.

The feeling of isolation from peers that Gen Z experienced during such formative years impacted their social skills and mental health. In a 'Mental Health Today' report by Deloitte in 2023, this generation reported high levels of stress and anxiety, driven by uncertainty about the future and social isolation. Many faced challenges entering the job market, with fewer opportunities and increased competition.

Meanwhile, for older Gen Zers, their first experiences of the workplace were working remotely, which influenced their expectations when the return to the office began. This has had a big impact on the ability to learn by osmosis, only gained when working alongside more experienced members of staff. This has affected their progress as well as their mental health – which this generation has continued to prioritise as they seek supportive environments and resources.

Expectations

Gen Zers expect transparency, authenticity and inclusivity in all areas of life. They want governments, employers and those around them to be socially responsible. They are looking to brands to take a stand on important issues, and politicians to prioritise the environment and social justice.

Like most generations before them at their age, they want to be heard and they want change, but what makes Gen Zers different is that they will be more forthright about vocalising their feelings. They're not afraid to call out hypocrisy or demand better. In the age of immediacy, they are less willing to wait for progression, pay rises and recognition. They are looking for a balance in their work and leisure time that older cohorts may suggest is unrealistic.

In the workplace, they expect clear communication, opportunities for growth and respect for their boundaries. Unlike previous generations, they're less willing to tolerate toxic work environments or rigid hierarchies. When it comes to expectations surrounding their careers, they are reshaping traditional pathways, particularly in industries that require years of training and experience before reaching leadership roles. Gen Zers are less inclined to wait decades for career milestones. In professions like medicine or law, where top positions are often only attained in one's late thirties or beyond, there may be growing tension between the traditional career ladder and Gen Z's desire for faster progression and immediate results. I have seen this in my old work environment of the cruise industry, where contract lengths and training times are being reviewed to attract the next generation to a career at sea. Other industries and organisations may also have to rethink how they structure career paths, offering earlier leadership opportunities, faster tracks for advancement or alternative ways to keep young talent engaged. If not, they risk losing ambitious Gen Z professionals to industries that are more agile and responsive to their expectations. This shift could lead to more innovative forms of training and development, but it also poses challenges in maintaining the depth of experience and expertise traditionally expected in such professions.

Financially, they expect a fair wage and opportunities to build wealth. Many are keenly aware of the economic challenges they face, from rising housing costs to student debt, and want systems that support their financial wellbeing.

Leisure

Leisure for Gen Z is often a blend of online and offline activities. Social media, streaming services and gaming are major pastimes, but they also value real-world experiences like travel, concerts and outdoor activities. For Gen Z, TV has undergone a significant shift compared to previous generations. While older generations grew up with terrestrial TV as the primary source of entertainment and information, young members of Gen Z have largely bypassed this medium in favour of digital and on-demand platforms. Instead of gathering around the TV for scheduled programming, they consume media on their own terms, often through smartphones, tablets and laptops. Platforms such as YouTube, TikTok and Instagram have become central to their lives, offering bite-sized, algorithm-driven content that caters to their interests. Streaming services such as Netflix and Disney+ also dominate their viewing habits, providing the flexibility to watch what they want, when they want. As a result, the communal viewing experience of traditional TV has given way to a highly personalised, fragmented media landscape where social media influencers and creators often hold as much, if not more, influence than traditional broadcasters.

Wellness is a big part of leisure time for Gen Zers, with many into fitness, meditation and healthy living. They're more likely to prioritise self-care and mental wellbeing than previous generations. They also enjoy creating content, whether it's through TikTok videos, YouTube channels or personal blogs. For them, leisure is often about creativity and self-expression as much as it is about relaxation.

Attitudes to money

Gen Zers have a cautious attitude towards money. Having seen their Millennial predecessors struggle with student debt and rising living costs, they're wary of taking on too much financial risk. Many prefer to save and invest early, with a focus on financial independence, somewhat different to older generations at the same age. In Britain, the high cost of living, especially in major cities, has made saving difficult for many young people. However, Gen Zers are more likely to seek out alternative ways to build wealth, such as investing in stocks, cryptocurrency and peer-to-peer lending platforms.

They value experiences over material possessions but are also keen on getting a good deal. They're more likely to spend on things that align with their values, such as sustainable fashion and eco-friendly products. This growing interest in sustainability and unique fashion has significantly contributed to the success of online second-hand clothing retailer Vinted, whose user base, according to an article in *The Guardian* (Butler 2024), has tripled between 2020 and 2024, with Gen Z driving seller activity. More and more Gen Zers are now earning money online, signalling a shift in how younger generations approach income generation and sustainability.

Summing up the accepted view of Gen Z

This cohort represents a profound generational shift, standing apart from its predecessors in almost every aspect of life. As the first true digital natives, they grew up in a world of constant connectivity, where technology and social media are as integral to their lives as electricity. Unlike Millennials, who recall a time before smartphones, Gen Zers have never known a world without them, shaping their values, communication styles and expectations. They are keenly aware of the world's challenges, from climate change to economic inequality, but determined to create change on their own terms. Diversity, inclusivity and authenticity are non-negotiable for them, and they demand the same from institutions and leaders. While they share some universal youthful traits, like a desire for fun and freedom, their approach is distinctly modern, valuing immediacy, purpose and adaptability. In redefining success, they prioritise personal growth and experiences over traditional milestones, making them a generation that both fascinates and challenges the world around them.

10 Generation Alpha

Born between 2012 and 2024

Like generational names in the 20th century, no team or group of experts got together to create a new name for the first generation that would be born entirely in the 21st century. As before, names emerge and then stick until they become common parlance. Australian social researcher Mark McCrindle coined the term Generation Alpha in 2005, seven years before its first members were even born. He chose the name because it follows the scientific convention of using the Greek alphabet. He also felt that it made sense to start with the letter 'alpha' instead of 'A' after ending with Gen Z and was inspired by the naming of hurricanes, which used Greek letters when the Latin alphabet ran out.

Who are they?

Although the oldest members of Generation Alpha are just entering their teenage years, they're already carving out a unique identity. Born into a world shaped by rapid tech innovation, environmental urgency and shifting social norms, their experience of childhood is distinctly different – even from Gen Z, just a few years ahead of them. These are true born-digital kids. Smart speakers, tablets and AI-driven devices have been part of their world from day one – as normal to them as Lego and Scalextric were to previous generations. Interactivity is second nature. They're engaged, hands-on learners who expect content to respond to them, not just talk at them. Maarten Leyts, author of *Generation ZAlpha* (2024), highlights their standout traits: adaptability, curiosity and a remarkable level of digital fluency, even at a young age

Gen Alphas are mostly the children of Millennials, and as McCrindle & Fell noted in *Generation Alpha* (2021), they already wield surprising brand influence and purchasing power. According to Leyts, they're not just consuming content – they're shaping the social media landscape and influencing pop culture, even before hitting secondary school.

In the UK, Gen Alphas are growing up in the shadow of climate change, rising awareness around social equality and mental health, and a growing emphasis on diversity. They're likely to become the most educated generation in history, with more information available to them than any previous cohort – and parents who are actively investing in quality education and structured activities. On one hand, Millennial parents seem keen to step back from the helicopter parenting they experienced themselves, aiming instead to strike a more balanced approach. Meanwhile, on the other, there's been a growing trend for 'tiger parenting' where, as McCrindle says in *Generation Alpha*, 'Parents drive academic success of their children through an authoritarian approach.'

What sets Gen Alpha apart isn't just the tech they use, but the world they're being raised in – one that prioritises inclusion, creativity and innovation. As they grow, they'll bring fresh perspectives to how we live, learn and work, just as every generation before them has. But if early signs are anything to go by, they'll do it with a global outlook, a swipe of a screen and a strong sense of who they are.

Notable figures

Considering their age, you may not expect many notable figures to have emerged for this generation, but there are rising stars, mostly on YouTube. Possibly the biggest rising star is Ryan Kaji (born 2011) who, with his parents, has built Ryan's World into a hugely successful empire. It all started as a series of toy reviews on YouTube and has now grown into a billion-dollar product line in Walmart. By the age of 12 – in August 2024 – Kaji already had ten YouTube channels, with billions of views totalling more than 57 million subscribers and a mobile game with more than 34 million downloads, and had just released his first movie, *Ryan's World the Movie: Titan Universe Adventure*. This has all added up to earnings of more than $35 million, according to *Forbes* (2024).

Young lives

For this generation, technology is almost a part of their DNA and childhood is a highly connected experience. In Britain, they're growing up with access to streaming services, on-demand content and interactive digital learning platforms. Play for this generation often involves a mix of physical and digital activities, from traditional toys to augmented reality games. Parents of this cohort are continuing the trajectory of what a 2024 report from the Ann and Robert H Lurie Children's Hospital of Chicago refer to as 'gentle parenting', which focuses on guiding children through decision-making processes without threats or punishments. This approach emphasises communication, empathy, respect and boundaries, fostering a partnership between parent and child. Millennial parents also often adopt a democratic style, encouraging open dialogue and celebrating their children's individuality. However, they are also somewhat overwhelmed by juggling work and family obligations, navigating conversations around mental health and all the advice on parenting from online platforms.

Social issues are more visible to Gen Alpha, thanks to the unavoidable impact of digital media. They're growing up in a world where conversations about diversity, equality and mental health are mainstream, and these values are likely to shape their perspectives as they mature.

Education

Generation Alphas are experiencing a much more personalised education thanks to tech-driven learning environments, with many schools integrating tablets, interactive whiteboards and online platforms into their teaching methods. A report in the UK *Parliament Post* (Vo & Webb 2024) suggested there is growing evidence that recent education trends have seen a greater emphasis on identifying neurodivergence at an early age, enabling more focused education.

The Covid-19 pandemic accelerated the use of virtual learning, giving Generation Alpha early exposure to remote education. This shift has led to greater familiarity with digital tools and platforms, which will likely benefit them in the future.

Continuing the trend of young Gen Zers, parents of Gen Alphas are highly involved in their children's education, often investing in private tutoring, extracurricular activities and enrichment programmes. There's also an increasing emphasis on soft skills, such as emotional intelligence and creativity, alongside traditional academic subjects.

This generation's formative years are also shaped by heightened environmental awareness. Many of them are learning about climate change from a young age and are encouraged to participate in sustainable practices such as recycling and reducing waste.

At work

Although at the time of writing Generation Alphas are far from entering the workforce, it's interesting that early indications already suggest they will have different expectations from previous generations (Dwyer 2025). Raised in a digital-first world, they're likely to seek jobs that offer flexibility, creativity and purpose. Automation and AI will play a significant role in defining their career paths, meaning many of the jobs they will do haven't even been invented yet.

They're expected to be highly entrepreneurial, much like their Gen Z predecessors. With early exposure to technology and innovation, many may choose to create their own opportunities rather than follow traditional career paths.

The Covid effect

For Gen Alphas born just before the pandemic, the inability to experience the social interactions that are so important in those first years will have a lasting impact on their emotional and social development. Those who were at early years school faced interruptions in their education, with remote learning impacting foundational skills. As reported in media outlets such as *The Guardian* (Weal et al 2025), the school closures and disrupted education resulted in developmental delays and increased reliance on technology among children. However, being so young, they showed remarkable adaptability, transitioning to virtual classrooms and finding new ways to play and connect with friends online. The pandemic also heightened Gen Alpha's awareness of health and hygiene, with many growing up in a world where masks, hand sanitiser and regular health checks became a normal part of life. This experience is likely to influence their long-term attitudes toward health and safety.

The impact on those born after 2021 will be much less, with just the legacy of the pandemic affecting their lives. Certainly, parents' experiences during the pandemic will have shaped Generation Alpha's environment, with increased focus on family dynamics and home life.

Expectations

Generation Alphas are likely to have high expectations when it comes to technology, education and societal progress. They're growing up in a world where instant access to information is the norm, and they will expect the same level of immediacy and convenience in other aspects of life. They're also likely to demand greater action on issues like climate change and social justice. Raised by socially conscious Millennials and Gen Xers, they're inheriting values that prioritise inclusivity, sustainability and mental wellbeing. They will also follow the trend of expecting employers, and the older generations, to increase inclusion, with a greater understanding of wellbeing and social issues.

Financially, they will expect more personalised and

digital-first banking solutions. With early exposure to financial literacy through apps and gamified learning, they're likely to be more financially savvy than previous generations.

Leisure

As you would expect, leisure for Generation Alpha is a blend of physical and digital experiences. While outdoor play and sports remain important, they also spend a significant amount of time engaging with digital content, from interactive games to educational apps. Streaming services, YouTube and social media platforms tailored to younger audiences play a central role in their leisure time. They're also drawn to creative activities, such as content creation and digital art.

Parents of Generation Alphas often prioritise well-rounded leisure activities, balancing screen time with physical exercise, family outings and hobbies like music or art. As they grow older, this generation is likely to continue blending digital and real-world experiences in unique ways.

Attitudes to money

Although it's early to gauge Generation Alpha's full attitude towards money, early trends suggest they will be highly financially literate. With access to financial education apps and digital piggy banks, they're learning about saving, spending and investing from a young age. They're also likely to prioritise value-driven spending. Raised by Millennials who value ethical consumption, Gen Alpha may place a greater emphasis on sustainability and social responsibility in their purchasing decisions.

Given the rise of digital currencies and alternative financial systems, Generation Alpha is expected to be comfortable with concepts like cryptocurrency, digital wallets and peer-to-peer payments.

Summing up the accepted view of Gen Alpha

Born into a world of rapid technological change and social transformation, members of Generation Alpha are poised to be highly adaptive, creative and socially conscious individuals. While they're still young, their early experiences with technology, education and global issues are already shaping their outlook.

As they grow, Gen Alpha will undoubtedly challenge norms, innovate and push for a better, more connected world. They represent the future that is digital, diverse and driven by a desire to make a positive impact. While at present it's only possible to speculate about their full potential, one thing is certain: Gen Alpha will leave their mark in ways we are only beginning to imagine.

How the generations really communicate

11 My generational communication surveys

One of the main objectives I had when setting out to write this book was to debunk some of the myths surrounding generational communication. I wanted to see how people across generations actually communicated, where patterns existed and where they didn't. I read numerous reports and surveys, but wanted to have some more neutral data, where the respondents would give me insights into their communication preferences without realising that I wanted to identify their generational differences. I decided to commission my own surveys through a respected survey company whose data would stand up to scrutiny. I started working with Dynata in the UK, who recommended Kate Thomson as a survey expert to help me formulate the questions. As a communications specialist, I decided that it would be my communications training company, Present Yourself, that would conduct the surveys, which would help with the neutrality of the responses.

Generations in the Workplace Study 2023

The purpose of the first survey, the Generations in the Workplace Study 2023, was to look at the impact of four generations in the workplace in Britain from an HR perspective. There is debate about how many generations are currently working, with some people suggesting there are five. However, I believe that while some people over 79 are still working, that number is very small, so it's only really four generations in the workplace in significant numbers. More specifically, my aim was to explore the extent to which HR managers in the UK see differences between the needs and expectations of different age groups within their workforce, and how they manage these.

Before diving into the details, it's helpful to understand a bit more about the survey itself and how it was conducted, as well as those who took part:

- **Number of respondents**: 110 HR professionals.

- **Industries represented**: Participants came from multiple sectors, including technology, healthcare, manufacturing, finance, retail and a handful of smaller niches. According to the respondents, their organisations ranged in size from fewer than 50 employees all the way up to several thousand employees.

- **Generations studied**: The survey focused primarily on the four generational cohorts currently in the workplace: Baby Boomers (born 1946–1964), Generation X (1965–1980), Millennials (Gen Y, 1981–1996) and Generation Z (1997–2011). Some respondents did mention a few Silent Generation (born before 1946) employees, but the survey data about them was minimal and did not form a core part of the results.

- **Survey format**: The survey included both quantitative (multiple-choice questions and rating scales) and qualitative (open-ended) questions. The goal was to capture not only numerical data but also real-world stories and specific examples that illustrate trends around generational communication.

Dynata carried out the survey online over a six-week period between July and August 2023. It received 110 responses from HR managers, with each survey taking an average of 11 minutes to complete.

Looking at the feedback, it was immediately clear that HR professionals agreed that having multiple generations on staff can be a great source of creativity and wide-ranging skill sets. At the same time, they also acknowledged that, if not managed carefully, conflicts in communication styles can complicate daily operations.

Their insights paint a nuanced picture of generational dynamics in the modern workplace, highlighting both challenges and opportunities for bridging the gap. The survey revealed a wide spectrum of perceptions. Broadly, HR professionals agreed that fostering better communication and understanding between generations is a pressing need. However, opinions varied significantly based on the respondents' age, industry and the size of their organisations.

I'll go into more detail on this survey in Chapter 18, 'The generations at work 1 – the view from HR', but its insights underscore the complexities of managing a multigenerational workforce. While challenges exist, the potential benefits of bridging generational gaps far outweigh the difficulties. By fostering open communication, challenging stereotypes and implementing tailored strategies, organisations can create workplaces that not only accommodate but celebrate generational diversity, as I discuss in Chapter 20.

One thing is clear: generational differences are not barriers but opportunities for growth, learning and innovation. It is up to leaders to harness this potential and pave the way for a truly cohesive workplace.

Communication Habits and Preferences Survey 2024

Following the successful Generations in the Workplace Study 2023 results, I realised there was a need to study different generations' communication preferences in more detail. I knew I needed a more in-depth and larger study of how individuals communicate. This meant asking six generations how they like to communicate, without them realising the study was generational. I also wanted to make sure I had some up-to-date data on Generation Alphas aged between 8 and 12 years old. This would provide valuable insights into the new emerging generation, who will start entering the workplace in 2030.

In the summer of 2024, I commissioned Dynata to conduct this second and far bigger communication survey and again, deliberately didn't mention anything about my generational research because I didn't want to affect people's mindsets as they responded to the survey.

Here is an overview of those who took part:

🏶 **Number of respondents**: 4,067 individuals

🏶 **Generations studied**: The survey had respondents from six generational cohorts:
- 235 Silent Generation (born before 1946)
- 911 Baby Boomers (1946–1964)
- 880 Generation X (1965–1980)
- 858 Millennials (Gen Y, 1981–1996)
- 982 Generation Z (1997–2011)
- 201 Generation Alpha (2012–2024)

🏶 **Survey format**: Just like the 2023 study, the survey included both quantitative (multiple choice, rating scale) and qualitative (open-ended) questions. The goal was to capture not only numerical data but also real-world stories and specific examples that illustrate trends around generational communication.

🏶 **Gender and socioeconomics**: There was even distribution between male and female and a broad spectrum across socioeconomic groups (see table below).

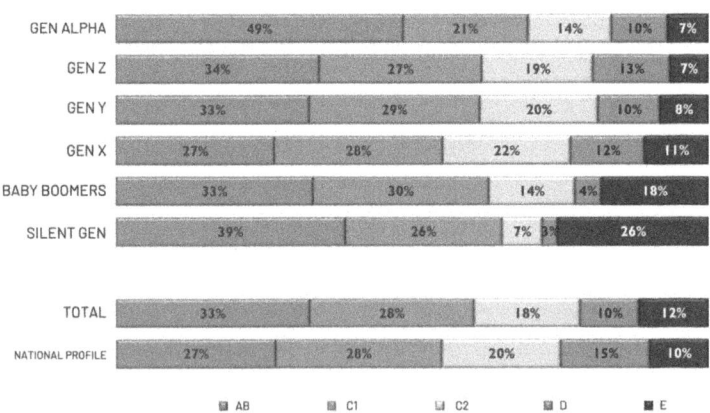

Communication Habits and Preferences Survey 2024: Breakdown of respondents by socioeconomic group (see NRS 2016 for definitions)

My aim was to get a snapshot of the way people in Britain communicated in 2024 with a completely open mind. I wasn't out to prove any particular result – I just wanted to understand how people felt and whether their responses matched the stereotypes projected by the media (more about that in Chapter 19). I deliberately set out to act as an observer so was keen not to ask any leading questions. Instead, I wanted to invite some open and honest views about how people communicate and how they perceive others from different generations.

Kate Thomson did an amazing job, working with me to put a survey together that would encompass all aspects of communication, with the view that we could do this again at regular intervals in the future to monitor trends. I asked Dynata to find respondents who would cover all age groups and in particular across social demographics. Few surveys in the past have covered such a widespread reach and even fewer have focused so much on the UK.

I will go into detail on the various sections of the survey in the next few chapters. Before I do, however, there were some initial questions asked only to over-16s that provided some very interesting insights.

The survey first asked respondents a few neutral questions, such as whether they enjoyed meeting new people and how they deal with things that go wrong. Overall, the survey sample was broadly spread in terms of approach to life, although the tendency to consider themselves a perfectionist fell away with age, while care to avoid jumping to conclusions increased.

The survey also asked the over-16s how well they thought they picked up on non-verbal communication such as body language. It was Gen Y (Millennials) who came out on top, with 33 per cent saying very well, with Gen X and Gen Z next at 26 and 27 per cent respectively.

Before talking about technology, the survey asked respondents how they interact with others and the generational nuances are interesting in that there weren't dramatic variations in the responses (see below). The biggest differences came with Gen Z, who were more likely to say they find it easier to communicate with people around their own age. They also stood out for liking to reach a decision carefully after weighing up many alternatives, which shows more considered thinking.

Easier to connect with people closer my own age

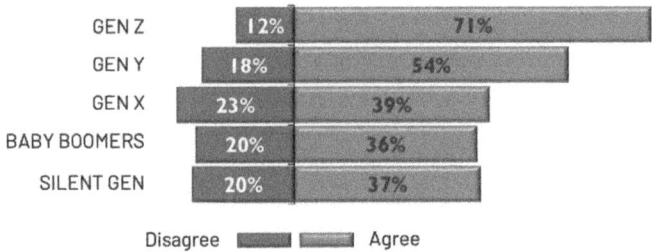

I like to reach a decision carefully after weighing up many alternatives

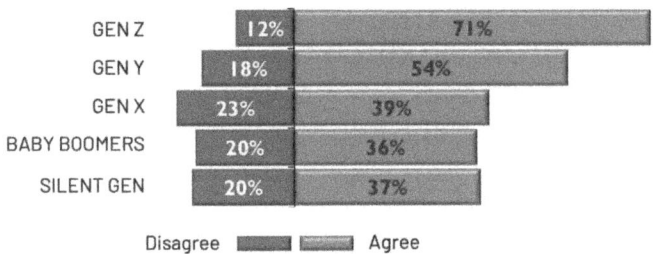

Good at organising people to get things done

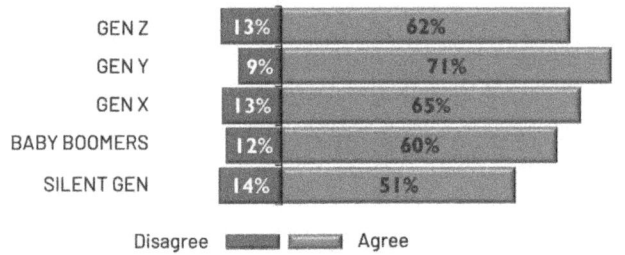

Interested to find out what others think

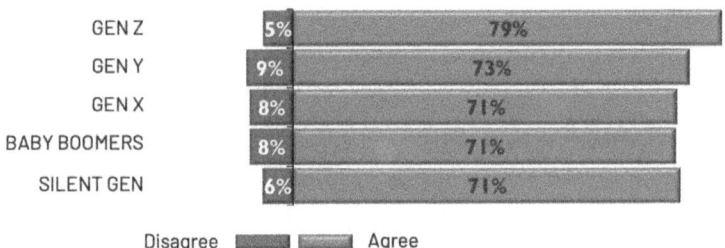

In discussions I like to get straight to the point

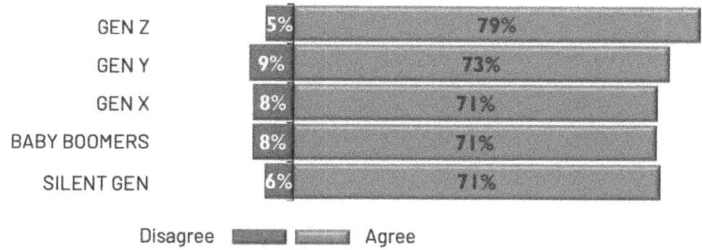

Disagree ▬▬ ▬▬ Agree

	Disagree	Agree
GEN Z	5%	79%
GEN Y	9%	73%
GEN X	8%	71%
BABY BOOMERS	8%	71%
SILENT GEN	6%	71%

Communication Habits and Preferences Survey 2024

This was just the beginning: there were lots more generational differences to find, which will be explored in the next few chapters.

From this data I have been able to gain some fascinating insights that I hope you'll be able to use regardless of what stage you are at in your career, and at whatever level of seniority. You'll find some great help and advice in Chapter 20.

12 The generations and technology

In a world shaped by constant digital innovation, the ways in which we adopt and adapt to technology reveal much about our habits, values and aspirations. The next section of the 2024 survey took a close look at technology use to discover how each generation incorporates devices, apps and online platforms into daily life. From smartphone ownership and online shopping to data privacy concerns, these findings illustrate both generational differences and common threads.

It would seem reasonable to think that generally the younger you are, the more adept you are using and interacting with technology. My study found that the picture is a lot more complex and there are nuances that defy the stereotypes. The survey first asked respondents how quick they were to try new things compared with people they knew.

I was surprised that even 11 per cent of the Silent Generation considered themselves early adopters and Gen Y (Millennials) were only 1 per cent behind Gen Z. However, while it enables communication across age groups, the ways different generations use and engage with technology vary significantly. Each generation, shaped by the era in which they grew up, has its own distinct relationship with digital tools. Some adopt new platforms seamlessly, while others approach them with scepticism, preferring to stick to tried and tested methods.

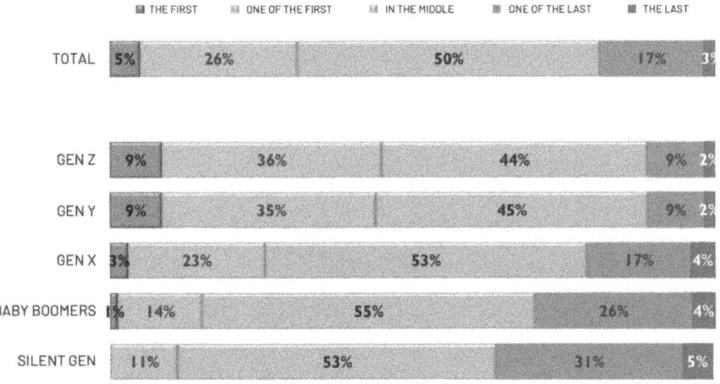

Communication Habits and Preferences Survey 2024: Respondents' willingness to try new things

Types of devices being used

The devices people choose to use are a reflection of their habits and comfort with technology. For younger generations, smartphones are an extension of themselves. 'I can't go anywhere without it,' remarked a Gen Z respondent, echoing the sentiment of millions. In my survey, 95 per cent of Gen Z owned a smartphone, although according to a report by GWI (Young 2025), that figure could be as high as 98 per cent worldwide. The survey revealed that 89 per cent of Millennials rely on their devices for both work and socialising. For the 8 to 12s, smartphones are not just a tool for communication but also an essential entertainment hub, with 76 per cent using them to watch videos, play games and interact on social media platforms.

In contrast, Baby Boomers (63 per cent) and the Silent Generation (45 per cent) remain more selective in their device use. Most have embraced smartphones – probably more than people may expect, with 79 per cent of the Silent Generation respondents to the survey owning one – but many still hold on to landlines and desktop computers, feeling they are simpler and more reliable. 'I like to keep things straightforward,' said a 75-year-old participant, explaining their continued preference for a traditional phone. The divide is particularly evident in professional settings, where younger generations expect instant messaging and mobile-friendly work environments, while older generations continue to prefer emails and calls made from office landlines.

Interestingly, while Gen X has largely moved to smartphones, 22 per cent still prefer desktops for everyday browsing, a habit that is much less common among younger generations. Laptops and desktops remain crucial for Gen X (53 per cent) and Millennials (59 per cent), particularly for work-related tasks. Tablets, however, have found their strongest foothold among Baby Boomers (37 per cent) and the Silent Generation (35 per cent), who appreciate their ease of use for reading and browsing the internet. 'I find a tablet much easier to hold than a laptop,' commented a 68-year-old respondent, who uses it primarily for reading news articles and checking email. Smartwatches and wearables, though growing in popularity, still face resistance from older generations. 'I don't see the need to check my messages on my wrist,' a Boomer noted, highlighting a common reluctance to adopt newer tech trends. However, Millennials and Gen Z have embraced these devices, often integrating them into their fitness routines and health monitoring.

Apps used by different generations

The apps people use provide a clear window into generational preferences. Social media illustrates this perfectly: Instagram is the most popular app with 42 per cent of all generations using it – mainly Gen Z and Millennials. Gen Alpha (25 per cent) and Gen Z (61 per cent) spend hours scrolling through TikTok, while Gen X (62 per cent) lean towards Facebook. 'Facebook is where my friends are,' a Gen X user explained, contrasting with a Gen Z respondent who dismissed it as 'for my parents'.

Messaging habits also differ. WhatsApp has managed to bridge generational gaps, with high usage among Gen X (80 per cent), Millennials (91 per cent), and Gen Z (87 per cent) but 16 to 21-year-olds are shifting towards Snapchat and TikTok, with many referencing Discord. 'I only check WhatsApp for family chats, but I talk to my friends on Discord,' noted a 17-year-old respondent.

Emoji and sticker use

The way people use emojis is almost a generational language in itself. Emojis, GIFs and stickers are an integral part of digital expression with Millennials (90 per cent) and Gen Z (91 per cent), who use them either all or some of the time. 'It's like adding tone to text,' said one Gen Z participant.

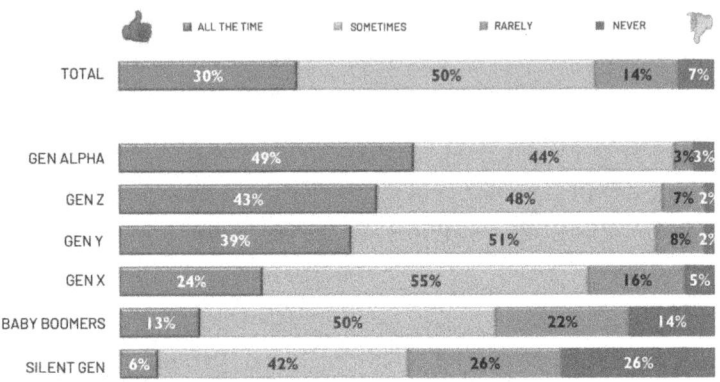

Communication Habits and Preferences Survey 2024: Respondents' use of emojis

However, older generations tend to stick to a more conservative set of symbols. 'A simple smiley face does the job,' noted a Baby Boomer.

Phone use for photos

The role of photography in daily life has evolved dramatically, with smartphones making it easier than ever to capture moments. Gen Z and Millennials (both 90 per cent) are the most prolific photographers, with many taking pictures daily, particularly of themselves. 'If I don't document it, did it even happen?' joked a Gen Z respondent, reflecting their attachment to social media. 'I prefer taking pictures of things that matter,' explained a Boomer, indicating a more traditional approach.

How generations pay for things

Payment preferences show a sharp generational divide that reflects each generation's use of technology. Contactless payments have become the norm for most generations, especially Millennials (88 per cent) and Gen Z (91 per cent). Cash use is definitely lower, probably accelerated by the pandemic, when card use was encouraged, but 17 per cent of the Silent Generation still rely more on cash. 'It's tangible; I know what I'm spending,' explained a Silent Generation respondent. The highest use of smartphones to pay was Gen Z (38 per cent), while only 1 per cent of Gen X and Gen Y (Millennials) pay by their watch or Fitbit.

Dating preferences for singles

In the survey, 344 respondents over the age of 18 identified their relationship status as single and dating. Asked how they were looking for dates, these respondents revealed very little difference overall between those who used online dating (58 per cent) and dating in social settings such as pubs and clubs (56 per cent). Referring to online dating, one Millennial explained, 'It's just how dating works now', while a Gen X respondent insisted, 'There's nothing better than meeting someone in real life.' Interestingly, 18 to 27-year-olds were the most likely to look for potential partners in their friendship groups. While the average percentage of those looking for dates among friends across all generations was 51 per cent, it was Gen Zers who were the highest at 61 per cent.

The use of AI platforms

At the time of the survey ChatGPT was less than two years old, but it was already making a huge impact on people's lives. Unsurprisingly, Gen Zers were leading the way with 59 per cent having used it at least once compared with only 13 per cent of Boomers. When it came to frequency of use, 29 per cent of Millennials were using it weekly as opposed to 28 per cent of Gen Z, probably because of the type of work they were involved in. Even 5 per cent of the 8 to 12-year-olds were already using it weekly.

Communication through online gaming

This was an interesting question for the younger generations, with 63 per cent of Gen Alpha communicating weekly through their gaming worlds. Gen Zers were quite a way behind on 41 per cent. Perhaps surprisingly, Gen Xers are also gaming, with 9 per cent communicating via gaming platforms on a weekly basis.

Summing up technology across generations

When it comes to the use of technology, as you would expect, the survey paints a vivid picture of generational differences. Having said that, across generations respondents clearly appreciate how technology – smartphones, WhatsApp, video calls, messaging apps – has made communication faster and more accessible, making it easy to stay connected with family and friends regardless of distance.

There are mixed reactions to how quickly technology is evolving, with some finding it exciting and others struggling to keep up. Some older generations can find the rapid pace of technological advancements difficult, with some feeling overwhelmed by the complexity and variety of communication platforms.

Younger generations eagerly embrace new platforms and payment methods, while older generations are a little more cautious – but not as much as some may suggest, according to the survey results. The gap between Gen Z and Millennials is narrowing in areas such as AI and digital payments, while Gen Alpha is understandably the most tech-native generation yet. Ultimately, while technology continues to evolve generational habits, fundamental differences remain in communication styles, payment preferences and engagement with digital trends.

13 Methods of communication

Communication has evolved dramatically over the past few decades, and our preferences for staying in touch are increasingly shaped by the technologies available to us. The findings from the survey provide a fascinating insight into how different age groups choose to connect, revealing clear generational patterns in communication methods, use of messaging platforms and acceptance of voice calls. While some of these patterns align with what you might expect, there are also surprising anomalies that challenge common assumptions.

How we wish each other 'happy birthday'

You may wonder why this question was asked, but I felt that one of the simplest indicators of communication preferences is how people choose to wish each other 'happy birthday'. This was a way of seeing how people communicate something quite simple but meaningful. At one time, the only way to do this was to send a birthday card in the post or make a telephone call. But now there are numerous options available to us, so which method did people choose?

		GEN ALPHA	GEN Z	GEN Y	GEN X	BABY BOOMERS	SILENT GEN
WhatsApp message	55%	53%	54%	70%	57%	46%	29%
Send a text	52%	47%	64%	53%	54%	40%	36%
Phone them	41%	38%	38%	39%	39%	46%	56%
Card in the post	39%	20%	13%	23%	45%	68%	79%
Instant message on social media	35%	23%	47%	43%	37%	21%	15%
Visit them in person	33%	54%	39%	31%	30%	29%	23%
Card via online service (eg Moonpig)	11%	4%	9%	11%	11%	11%	14%
Email	11%	2%	4%	7%	11%	19%	36%
Voice note	11%	25%	20%	15%	5%	2%	0%

Communication Habits and Preferences Survey 2024: Methods of wishing friends and family a happy birthday

According to the survey, younger generations overwhelmingly and unsurprisingly opted for digital methods. Gen Z and Millennials were most likely to send a WhatsApp message, an instant message on social media or a text. In contrast, Baby Boomers (46 per cent) and the Silent Generation (56 per cent) were more inclined to pick up the phone and call their loved ones. A 67-year-old Baby Boomer shared: 'There's something special about hearing someone's voice rather than reading a message on a screen.'

A significant proportion of older generations are sending birthday cards. Compare 79 per cent of the Silent Generation who would post a card with just 13 per cent of Gen Z. Younger respondents were far more pragmatic, with one 24-year-old saying: 'A quick message is just as thoughtful. It's how we communicate now.'

A topic for a future survey could be how we like to receive birthday wishes. When I was first studying generational differences, I heard about a 12-year-old who would never dream of sending a card to someone unless prompted by a parent. However, their own face beamed with excitement when a card appeared on the doormat. This suggests that things are more nuanced than a survey could ever reveal.

Another trend that has emerged over the past few years is the concept of messaging people before calling them. Ten years ago, I certainly would never have thought about scheduling a call first, but when I conducted a poll on LinkedIn in 2024, 29 per cent of the 484 respondents said they message beforehand most of the time, while 34 per cent said sometimes and only 18 per cent never. This insight matters if we want a call to go positively as opposed to being considered impolite for not scheduling it first.

The disappearance of personal letters

Asked when they last sent a personal letter or handwritten note, the responses painted a stark generational divide. More than 43 per cent of Gen Z and 65 per cent of Millennials confirmed they had not sent a letter in the past year, with some respondents never having done so in their lifetime. In contrast, Baby Boomers and the Silent Generation still engage with letter writing occasionally, often for formal occasions or heartfelt messages. One Silent Generation respondent commented: 'A handwritten letter shows care and effort – something a quick email or message can never replicate.' However, for younger generations, the convenience of digital communication outweighs senti-mentality. 'Why wait days for a letter when you can send an instant message in seconds?' remarked a 31-year-old Millennial. But letter writing is dying out for all generations, with 28 per cent of Gen X saying they hadn't sent one in the past year.

Preferred methods for keeping in touch with friends and family

Across all generations, messaging platforms dominate communication with friends and family. However, the platform of choice varies by age. WhatsApp is the most widely used app for personal communication across all age groups, particularly among Gen X, Millennials and Baby Boomers. Gen Zers, however, lean more towards social media messaging apps such as Instagram DMs and Snapchat.

It's just the Silent Generation who remain loyal to phone calls, with 47 per cent stating that their primary way of reaching out to loved ones is through a direct call. One respondent from the Silent Generation noted, 'A phone call is more meaningful. You can hear emotion and have a proper conversation.'

	GEN ALPHA	GEN Z	GEN Y	GEN X	BABY BOOMERS	SILENT GEN
WhatsApp message	38% / 41%	35%	49%	42%	34%	21%
Phone them	25% / 19%	19%	22%	21%	33%	47%
Text Them	18% / 14%	23%	13%	22%	16%	12%
Instant message on social media	8% / 7%	14%	9%	6%	4%	4%
Email them	4% / 2%	2%	2%	4%	9%	12%
Visit in person	3% / 9%	3%	3%	4%	2%	3%
Send a voice note	1% / 3%	3%	1%	1%	0%	0%

Communication Habits and Preferences Survey 2024: Methods of staying in touch with others

Within this context, we must consider how phone usage varies for younger respondents, with parental controls for this age group varying significantly from one household to another. Some of the Gen Alpha group did not have the same continuous access to personal devices as others. Consequently, these Gen Alpha participants sometimes find themselves out of the loop if a teacher or classmates rely heavily on, say, a smartphone app for announcements. One Gen Alpha wrote, 'My mum won't let me have WhatsApp till I'm older, so I sometimes don't know when the after-school club is cancelled!' This reveals a counterpoint to the assumption that all young learners are constantly plugged in.

Although voice notes are gaining in popularity, especially with Gen Z and Gen Alpha, only 3 per cent use them as a main way of contacting others. Looking at frequency of communication, some striking generational patterns emerged. Text messages (SMS) and WhatsApp messages are used frequently by all generations, but most commonly by Gen X, with more than 53 per cent stating that they send texts at least once a day. Even 32 per cent of Silent Generation respondents are sending more than one message a day.

Older generations are also learning from younger family members. I recall many years ago, when my then 20-year-old niece was working in China, that the only way her grandmother could get in touch was to learn how to use the best platform at the time, which was Skype. In this survey a Baby Boomer wrote:

'I used to always phone people to get a quick answer, but now I see that texting is more polite. My grandchildren taught me that.' This shift underlines how generational lines aren't always hard and fast, as life circumstances, family influences and personal curiosity can spur changes in habit.

Emails seem to be used predominantly for work or formal communication, with 37 per cent of Baby Boomers and 29 per cent of Gen X being the most frequent email users, sending multiple emails a day. While Gen Zers are still using email, the frequency drops to just 10 per cent sending multiple emails each day.

Although not the primary method of communication, the rise in popularity of voice notes is noticeable among younger generations, with 20 per cent of Gen Z sending more than one a day compared to just 2 per cent of Baby Boomers. A 26-year-old commented: 'Voice notes let you say more without typing, and they feel more personal.' However, an anomaly emerged with Gen Alphas who, despite their young age, are already showing strong adoption of voice notes. A parent of an 11-year-old commented: 'My child sends voice notes all the time – it's like their version of a phone call.' I believe we will probably see this number grow across all generations.

Do people like talking on the phone?

Many older people complain that younger people don't talk on the phone – it's one of today's hot topics. The data from the survey found that while 49 per cent of Baby Boomers and 62 per cent of the Silent Generation use the phone a lot, there is a marked drop among the younger generations, for all of whom the figure is around 35 per cent. A 22-year-old respondent admitted: 'I'll avoid a call if I can. Texting is just easier.' The perception about Generation Z's lack of enthusiasm for using the phone seems to hold up, but the reasons are probably more nuanced. Not only were they not brought up talking on the phone like previous generations, but it's also not something they need to do with so many alternatives. As telephone communication specialist Anthony Stears told me on my *Generationally Speaking* podcast, 'Younger people aren't scared of the phone — they're scared of getting it wrong,' adding, 'Gen Z do their homework before calling — they research, they stalk, they prep.'

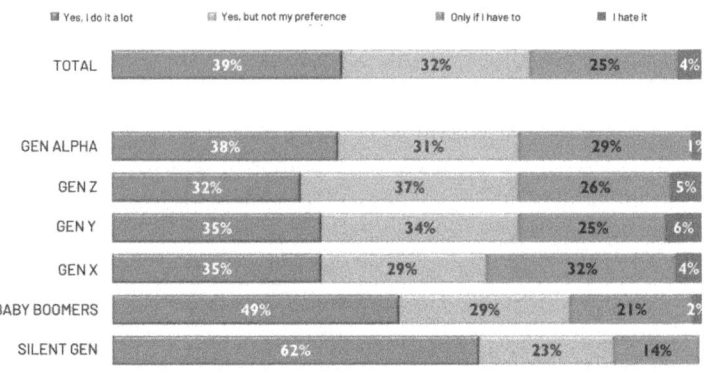

Communication Habits and Preferences Survey 2024: Generational phone use

Although Gen Zers were the most reluctant in the survey, the issue is clearly bigger than just one generation.

This reluctance extends to answering calls from unknown numbers. Only 69 per cent of all those surveyed were prepared to answer such calls. Gen X and Baby Boomers are more likely to pick up a call from an unknown number. As one 65-year-old noted, 'You never know if it's important.'

It's interesting to observe what happens when someone makes a call and the other person doesn't pick up. The generational response varies significantly, with only 12 per cent of Gen Zers prepared to leave a voicemail compared with 28 per cent of Gen Xers or 46 per cent of Baby Boomers. The number of survey respondents who would try again later was about the same, but the younger generations were more likely to send a text or message, with 53 per cent of Gen Zers suggesting this is what they would do. In contrast, Baby Boomers and the Silent Generation were more likely to redial until they got through. One 59-year-old Gen X respondent humorously stated: 'If my kids don't answer, I'll send a text. If they don't reply, I know they're ignoring me!'

Summing up methods of communication

The results of the survey reinforce the idea that communication is in a constant state of evolution. While older generations value direct voice interactions and written communication, younger generations lean heavily towards digital and instant messaging. A 2023 study by mobile provider Three UK found that 58 per cent of Gen Z individuals feel nervous making calls to unfamiliar people, and 47 per cent of 16 to 24-year-olds prefer texting over answering calls. Additionally, 40 per cent of young people ask others to make calls on their behalf to avoid doing it themselves. This would suggest a decline in traditional communication skills, but the survey finding was that although this is broadly the case, the picture is far more nuanced. For example, voice notes are bridging the gap between phone calls and texting, and some younger people still appreciate the thoughtfulness of traditional communication methods. The comments received in the survey suggest that many people think technology has made us lazy and our communication today more transactional. Some miss the personal connection that comes with phone calls and face-to-face interactions, with over-reliance on tech leading to a potential loss of social skills or emotional depth in communication.

The way we communicate may differ, but at its core, the goal remains the same: staying connected. We just have more choice today. As technology continues to evolve, it will be interesting to see how these preferences shift in the coming years.

14 The generations and social media

Social media has become an intrinsic part of our daily communication, influencing how we connect, share and engage with others. Its impact on all generations, but in particular the young, cannot be underestimated. The topic is the source of numerous conversations at home, school, work and in social settings and was one area I was keen to get some current data on. I wanted to see how people across generations use social media today and how they differed from each other and from common perceptions.

To a certain degree I could have predicted that the way different generations interact with social media would vary significantly according to the age when they first encountered it. As I've discussed before, the impact has been the greatest for the young, who have been shaped by early exposure to technology, parental influence and societal influences. The survey reveals a range of insights that have highlighted patterns, unexpected anomalies and generational shifts in digital engagement.

Who's online and how often?

It is no surprise that social media usage is high across all generations; there will be few who are not impacted by its reach. However, the intensity and purpose of engagement differ according to age. Gen Zers were the most frequent users, with more than 91 per cent confirming they use social media daily. This was followed by Millennials at 86 per cent, while even 69 per cent of Gen X engage with social media daily. However, Baby Boomers and the Silent Generation show a split in habits. While some are avid users, others either engage less frequently or avoid social media altogether. One Baby Boomer respondent commented, 'I check in a few times a week, but I don't feel the need to be online all the time.'

The survey also revealed that Gen Alpha is already deeply immersed in social media, with parental supervision shaping their habits and the amount of time spent on it. A parent of a ten-year-old noted: 'My child knows more about social media than I do, and they're not even a teenager yet.' I'll look more at this age group in Chapter 16.

When the survey respondents were asked how much time they spend on social media daily, the results showcased clear generational divides.

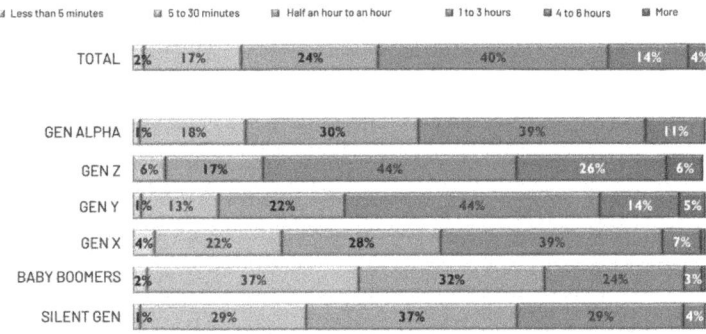

Communication Habits and Preferences Survey 2024: Time spent on social media

The most prolific social media users are Gen Zers, with 44 per cent spending an average of one to three hours per day online. More than a quarter spend between four and six hours on socials with 6 per cent spending more than six hours a day. Millennials are close to those figures, but it's striking to see how much the older generations are spending on social media.

Perhaps it's because of the spare time retirement affords, but 29 per cent of the Silent Generation are spending between one and three hours on social media – that's more than Baby

Boomers. One Silent Generation respondent noted: 'I log in to see what my grandchildren are up to, but I don't stay for long.' In contrast, a 25-year-old from Gen Z admitted: 'I'll go on for five minutes and end up staying for an hour.' It will be interesting to see how these figures change in the future – I predict that we will see older generations spending an increasing amount of time on social media platforms. The big question is, which platforms?

The way different generations engage with social media also varies. Gen Zers lead in active engagement, frequently liking, reposting and sharing content. More than 60 per cent of Gen Z respondents interact with posts multiple times a day, while Baby Boomers and the Silent Generation are far more passive, with many stating they rarely interact with content beyond viewing it. One 67-year-old noted: 'I scroll and read, but I don't feel the need to like or comment on everything.' Meanwhile, a 19-year-old Gen Z respondent said: 'Social media is all about interaction. If I like something, I want people to know it.'

Posting habits reveal another fascinating split. Gen Z and Millennials are the most frequent content creators, with more than 50 per cent posting at least once a week and some multiple times a day. Gen X, Baby Boomers and the Silent Generation are more reserved, with the majority posting only occasionally or not at all.

The greatest indication of the way a generation thinks could be to look at the reasons they are posting content on social media. So what are people posting? You can see in the table below the most commonly shared content across all generations.

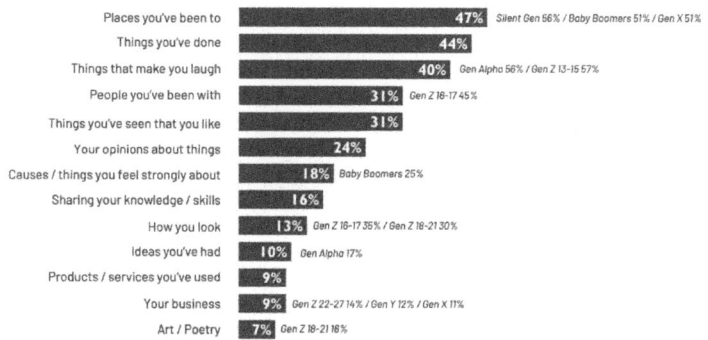

Communication Habits and Preferences Survey 2024: What respondents are posting on Instagram

The fact that places you've been to comes out top shows how the world has changed from a more material to an experiential one – and this is across all generations. On a holiday to Bali in 2024, we were offered the 'Instagram' tour of the island we were visiting, Nusa Penida. Interestingly, our taxi driver told us the island's tourist industry had expanded rapidly in the previous few years because of Instagram beauty spots like Bunga Mekar. Perhaps a reason for older generations posting more in this area is their ability to travel more. Now I knew *what* people post on social media I wanted to find out *why* they were posting.

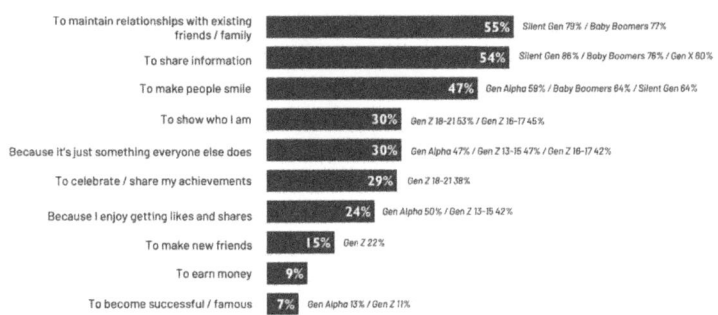

To maintain relationships with existing friends / family	55%	Silent Gen 79% / Baby Boomers 77%
To share information	54%	Silent Gen 86% / Baby Boomers 76% / Gen X 60%
To make people smile	47%	Gen Alpha 59% / Baby Boomers 64% / Silent Gen 64%
To show who I am	30%	Gen Z 18-21 53% / Gen Z 16-17 45%
Because it's just something everyone else does	30%	Gen Alpha 47% / Gen Z 13-15 47% / Gen Z 16-17 42%
To celebrate / share my achievements	29%	Gen Z 18-21 38%
Because I enjoy getting likes and shares	24%	Gen Alpha 50% / Gen Z 13-15 42%
To make new friends	15%	Gen Z 22%
To earn money	9%	
To become successful / famous	7%	Gen Alpha 13% / Gen Z 11%

Communication Habits and Preferences Survey 2024: Why respondents post on social media

As you can see from the chart, Gen Z and Millennials often post for engagement, with more than 40 per cent citing likes and shares as motivation. 'It's nice to get reactions. It feels like validation,' said one 22-year-old. Meanwhile, for older generations, the motivation is more about connection and information sharing. 'I post updates about my life because it helps me stay in touch with friends and family,' said a 58-year-old Gen X respondent.

If you look behind the statistics at what is being posted and by which generation, you get an idea of what is motivating them to be on social media – and here it gets interesting, because there are some anomalies. One of these is the number of passive social media users among Gen Z. While many young users are highly engaged, some prefer a 'silent observer' approach, consuming content without actively interacting. Another anomaly, looking at some of the comments, is that it seems Baby Boomers are embracing social media for news consumption, reporting using it primarily to stay informed. 'I follow news pages more than I follow people,' noted a 66-year-old respondent. For younger users, while social media is a popular source of entertainment, they seem to be moving away from highly public profiles, opting instead for closed groups and private messaging apps.

One of the most frequently voiced concerns in our conversations across generations (especially from parents, educators and older respondents) is the impact of social media on young people. The anxiety is palpable. Many parents of Gen Z and Generation Alpha children express fears around exposure to harmful content, cyberbullying and the addictive nature of platforms designed to keep users endlessly scrolling. As one Baby Boomer put it in the survey, 'We wouldn't dream of letting our children walk alone down a dangerous street, but we hand them a phone that opens the world without knowing what they're stepping into.' This supports the view of Jonathan Haidt in *The Anxious Generation* (2024) that we are being 'over-protective in the real world and underprotective in the digital world'. This sense of unease is echoed by schools, which are increasingly having to respond to the fallout – mental health struggles, lack of focus and peer pressure amplified to a whole new level.

Teachers and school leaders are particularly alert to the way social media influences not only behaviour but also communication style. They see students more comfortable with emojis and TikTok trends than with face-to-face conversation. Social media expert Mark Saxby, who works extensively in schools, told me on my *Generationally Speaking* podcast: 'One headteacher told me 95 per cent of school issues were caused by social media.' Working with his Positive Social charity, which helps young people to survive and thrive on social media, he has a simple message: 'We don't tell kids to quit social media – we teach them how to use it right.' He also has advice for parents: 'Your kids watch your phone habits – they copy what you do, not what you say.'

There's also a growing worry that while social media enables constant contact, it may be eroding real connection. One Gen X respondent, a secondary school teacher, noted: 'They message each other constantly but seem lonelier than ever.' The question isn't just whether young people are spending too much time online, but what that time is doing to their sense of identity, self-worth and ability to relate to others in the real world. This tension between digital connection and emotional disconnection sits at the heart of the generational communication gap – and it's one that urgently needs attention.

Social media continues to evolve, and generational preferences reflect broader trends in technology adoption and digital behaviour. While younger generations use it as a primary mode of communication and self-expression, older generations approach it with more caution, using it selectively to connect and stay informed. Regardless of age, one thing is clear: social media is now embedded in everyday life.

15 Communications at school and university

Half of Generation Z are currently in education, whether that's at school, college or university, and it's only by 2033 that nearly all of them will be in the workplace (Bolton 2025). Because of this, for some questions Generation Z was split into narrower groups. For example, when asked where they felt more productive, the survey showed that younger Gen Zers have different values and attitudes from older members of the same generation. This is one example that shows why it's important to understand the type of employees who will start walking through workplace doors in the coming years.

In my Communication Habits and Preferences Survey 2024, 386 respondents were under 16 and 314 of those over 16 were full-time students. A further 19 had been in full or part-time education in the previous 12 months. Of this total, 42 per cent were doing a degree course and the remaining respondents were at school or sixth-form college.

All students were asked how they primarily communicate with peers at school or university. Of the respondents, 61 per cent of Gen Zers and 47 per cent of Gen Alphas said they used school-related platforms to talk to teachers and classmates, with only 19 per cent saying they don't really like that method of learning and communication. A Gen Alpha pupil commented: 'We have class iPads and the teacher checks them once a week, but I still talk face-to-face with friends. We don't really message each other in class unless we have to research something.'

Schools, colleges and universities have always been at the forefront of generational change. They bring together young people who are naturally immersed in new tools of communication with academics and older staff members who might adapt over time. The survey showed a broad consensus among respondents that the tools students now use to engage with classmates and teachers have shifted dramatically compared to a decade or two ago. The majority of participants (including some who identified as lifelong learners or mature students still in the education system) reported that technology plays a major role in the day-to-day educational experience. A 12-year-old wrote: 'My teacher set up a shared drive so we can swap ideas for our projects. I like it better than handwriting everything, but she sees all our messages!' That watchful eye may limit spontaneity, but it also nurtures digital literacy.

However, the amount that technology is used in schools isn't consistent, with one 16 to 17-year-old observing: 'Education in all aspects is behind the real world, but especially in communication – reception still communicates with students via paper notes handed out by other students.'

Where do students feel more productive?

Over-16s were then asked where they felt most productive. Their answers showed an interesting divide.

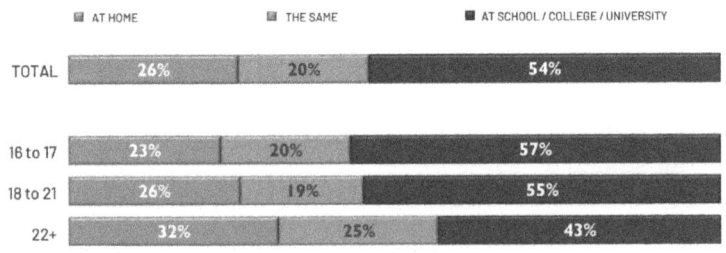

Communication Habits and Preferences Survey 2024: Where do respondents feel more productive

Face-to-face communication remains the preferred method of learning for 54 per cent of all students, with one 18 to 21-year-old commenting: 'Needs more personal communication between individual and lecturer.' Only 26 per cent reported feeling they are more productive at home, although 32 per cent of students over 22 found their home environment more productive.

How do students prefer to communicate?

When over-16s were asked how they would get hold of fellow students, unsurprisingly messaging was most popular, with 46 per cent choosing to instant message on social media. Only 37 per cent would go and see someone in person and only 26 per cent would pick up the phone and call their friends. Interestingly, email for this generation is even lower at just 18 per cent, although it's slightly higher (22 per cent) for those over 22 years old. A Gen Zer wrote: 'I rely on group chats and Discord to keep track of project updates. It's so much faster than email, and I feel more connected to my classmates.'

But students are pragmatic and understand they need to adapt their preferred style to get a message understood by people of different generations, as one 18-year-old told us: 'I'm used to texting friends if we need to meet after school, and we have a group chat for exam revision. When it's official stuff like asking a teacher for an extension, I still use email because they reply faster that way.'

When it comes to phone usage at schools, I was surprised to read that 55 per cent of under-16s who have a mobile phone of their own are allowed to use it at school, although this was less for Gen Alpha at 43 per cent. Thirty-two per cent said they could use their phone at breaks and lunchtime while 19 per cent said they could use them for emergencies only. Surprisingly, 4 per cent said there were no restrictions at all. I say surprisingly, because generally, and certainly in my experience in schools, most children study in strictly controlled environments where devices can be confiscated during class. School bans exist in most of the schools I've been in, with policies that have evolved to become increasingly strict, especially since the pandemic. In 2025, eight months after my survey, a report by the UK

Children's Commissioner said that 90 per cent of secondary schools and 99.8 per cent of primary schools now have policies in place that stop the use of mobile phones during the school day. The report also went on to add that a nationally representative poll of children in England aged 8 to 15 also found that 25 per cent spend two to three hours a day using an internet-enabled device such as a computer, smartphone, tablet or gaming console, while 23 per cent spend more than four hours a day on such a device.

Video calls are generally not popular in the context of education and learning. Whether this is due to the legacy of the pandemic or something else, I don't know, but it will be interesting to see how this changes in future years. In my survey, more than 25 per cent of those under the age of 22 still in education reported hating video calls (the highest for those aged between 16 and 22), but at the same time, 17 per cent of this age group said they enjoy them.

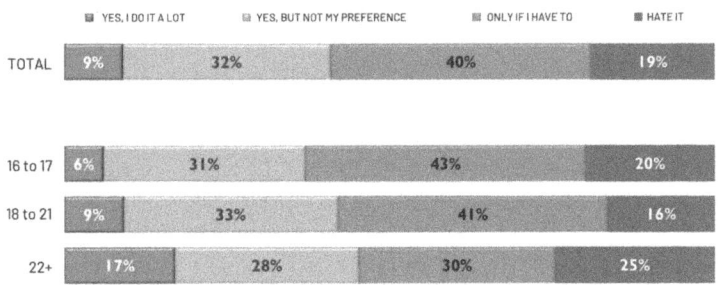

Communicating by video call in the context of education and learning

It seems that as students get older, they develop stronger preferences one way or the other, with only just over 30 per cent ambivalent about video calls by the age of 22. Universities and colleges also vary, so the student experience can be quite different from place to place, with some students telling us they have to rely heavily on face-to-face check-ins with lecturers. One Gen Z participant wrote: 'My college is surprisingly old-fashioned about communication. We have group chats, but tutors hardly reply unless it's through formal email. So, we're juggling both worlds.'

Perhaps employers who will be seeing these students

entering the workplace in the next year or so should consider an omnichannel approach to communication – something I'll talk about more in Chapter 20.

What do students feel about feedback?

Feedback is probably one of the most talked about subjects in the workplace today when it comes to younger generations – which is why it's valuable to learn about the next cohort to enter the workplace. The survey first asked students over 16 to consider how often they would like feedback on their performance from teachers or tutors. As predicted, 'as often as possible' was most popular at 26 per cent – although this seems to indicate weekly (also at 26 per cent), as only 6 per cent wanted feedback daily. Among 16 to 17-year-olds, 33 per cent wanted feedback as often as possible. Monthly feedback doesn't cut it for our younger generations, with only 16 per cent feeling this was about right for them.

The survey then asked how often they actually get feedback from teachers or tutors, and this revealed a startling disparity. Only 11 per cent are receiving more frequent feedback than they would like, with a huge 60 per cent of student respondents saying they are getting feedback less often than they would like. The good news is that this is being partially recognised by teachers and tutors of 16 to 17-year-olds, as 30 per cent of this age group said they do in fact receive weekly feedback. What is really striking is that 26 per cent of 18 to 21-year-olds reported they are only receiving feedback every three months, so it's easy to see why so many students feel let down.

Summing up communications at school and university

Far from a straightforward digital revolution among the youngest cohorts, the data paints a very mixed picture where students' expectations are often not met. This should be essential reading for all educational establishments to help them connect more effectively with their students. While every generation may bring unique preferences and experiences to the table, successful communication – be it in a school environment or a multinational organisation – often arises from the willingness to blend the best of various methods. Emails and phone calls still coexist with chat apps, video calls and social media channels, each tailored to the type of message and the relationship between the people exchanging it.

Education, by virtue of assembling these generations under a shared goal, underscores how adaptability and mutual respect for different styles can forge a more inclusive and effective communication culture.

Meanwhile, the 8 to 12-year-old Gen Alphas who answered the survey are indeed rapid adopters of real-time messaging platforms, social media groups and collaboration tools. The way they interact with technology can be limited by school education style preferences, device policies and parental oversight. I'll investigate this further in the next chapter.

16 Introducing Generation Alpha

With the first Generation Alpha babies born in 2012, it's still early days to start predicting how this generation will communicate and interact with others. However, my study managed to survey more than 200 youngsters between the ages of 8 and 12 to get an idea of how what I call the 'AI generation' is thinking. With the oldest making the big life stage move into secondary school in 2023, the youngest have only just been born. Those in business might be wondering why this generation is important to understand, but remember that in just a few years this generation will start entering the workplace and their communication preferences today are likely to be reflected in what they will expect when they get there.

The survey gave a snapshot of the oldest third of the generation (aged 8 to 12) and although these respondents only answered some of the survey questions, it has still been possible to glean some fascinating insights. This is a generation that is growing up in a world where digital tools coexist with traditional classroom methods.

When it comes to access to technology, while 98 per cent of 13 to 15-year-olds answering the survey said they have smartphones, only 67 per cent of 8 to 12-year-olds had one. Just 1.5 per cent of 8 to 12-year-olds had phones that weren't smartphones and of those who had smartphones 73 per cent first got one when they were aged ten or younger. The responses from Gen Alphas revealed a generation that values face-to-face conversation as much as it does tablets and messaging apps. They commented in the survey that their tech usage is often filtered through parents, teachers or school policies, which shape how and when they communicate.

Looking more closely at this 8 to 12-year-old group revealed that they tended to view technology with curiosity and enthusiasm. Many also reported using school tablets or a single, teacher-managed digital platform rather than having complete access to personal devices. According to one ten-year-old: 'We have iPads at school for research, but the teacher checks them every day. It's cool, but I wish I could take mine home so I could learn new apps on my own.' Comments like this point to Gen Alpha's eagerness for digital exploration, even if it is constrained by adult rules.

This generation's tech habits emerge partly from their environment. Some 48 per cent of Gen Alpha respondents said they use a personal smartphone or tablet at least once a week for communication, a figure well below older cohorts but significant for children under strict supervision.

Face to face first

Despite assumptions that these children are glued to screens, the survey data underscores that most Gen Alpha respondents still rely on in-person communication for everyday chat. When it comes to school, 60 per cent said face-to-face discussions with teachers are their top choice for clarifying questions – higher than any digital method.

They find talking at break or after school the simplest route, mainly because not everyone in this age bracket has a phone. One nine-year-old said, 'I always ask my friend stuff in person. We're not allowed to have phones at school, and my parents won't let me have mine overnight.' Another eight-year-old exclaimed, 'We love playing together in the playground – no phone can beat that!'

So, while technology is important, Generation Alpha does not yet regard it as a default for day-to-day conversation. For many, it is a tool for specific situations such as finishing group homework or checking their teacher's webpage for an assignment.

Early collaboration and email

In this survey, questions specific to Gen Alpha revealed that children use email to contact teachers about homework queries, school clubs or test schedules. This is usually because their schools encourage them to practise formal writing. A ten-year-old quipped: 'My teacher says emailing is a life skill. I only send emails for class or if I need permission for a trip.' Another, age 12, observed: 'I'd rather text my teacher, but we're not allowed. We have to email, so she can keep track.'

Some kids mentioned using online collaboration platforms during group assignments. One 11-year-old said: 'We used Google Docs for our science project, so we didn't have to be in the same room. I liked that we could edit at the same time.' Even so, this is far from universal. Many children said their schools lack resources or that teachers prefer pencil-and-paper activities.

Parental and adult influence

Another statistic to come out of the survey was that 63 per cent of older Gen Alphas said there are rules at home for when and how they use their phone. An 11-year-old said: 'My mum sets a timer on my tablet. If I run out of minutes, I can't text my best friend about the homework. It's annoying, but I get why she does it.' However, 24 per cent said there are rules just sometimes and, perhaps worryingly, 10 per cent said there are no rules at all. In her book *There's Still No Such Thing as Naughty* (2024), Kate Silverton warns: 'Your cellphone has already replaced your camera, your calendar, your alarm clock – don't let it replace your family.' It's a cautionary message to every parent.

Because most Gen Alpha children are under direct adult supervision, parents and teachers shape much of their communication style. An eight-year-old mentioned: 'If my dad sees me on YouTube for too long, he'll take away my iPad for the rest of the day. So, I'm careful about what apps I open.' Another

12-year-old recounted: 'My mum sits with me when I message my cousins. She checks who I'm talking to.'

Some children cite older siblings' influence. A nine-year-old explained: 'My brother is 14 and can do what he wants on his phone. I can't wait until I'm that old!' Meanwhile, a 10-year-old shared: 'My sister showed me how to record videos. Now I can send them to my grandparents if Mum's OK with it.' These snapshots suggest that older relatives, who often belong to Gen Z, can pass down digital know-how. But most Gen Alphas still operate within rules set by adults, so they can't explore technology quite as freely.

Gen Alphas are also keeping their parents in check – as much if not more so than previous generations. Because of their access to social media, they have formed opinions at an early age. Emma, a Millennial friend of mine, was talking to her 12-year-old daughter about decorating their house and was told: 'As long as you don't decorate it in that awful Millennial grey' – referring to the grey colour palette that was popular in home furnishings in the early 2020s. And so, each generation continues to stamp its mark on the next.

Attitudes towards social media

Social media usage in Gen Alpha is limited: fewer than 10 per cent use mainstream platforms openly, largely because of age restrictions and parental rules. While some older children (11 or 12) might dabble in safe versions of social apps or have group chats with friends, most in this age range either lack personal smartphones or have heavily restricted usage. They often rely on parents or older siblings to guide them. A nine-year-old explained: 'Sometimes I see my older sister using Instagram or TikTok, but I'm not allowed on them yet. I want my own apps, but my mum says I have to wait.'

Those children who do have some access often mentioned using family shared accounts or teacher-supervised forums. A 12-year-old wrote: 'I have TikTok, but I'm only allowed to post dance videos my mum approves first.' In a separate comment, a 10-year-old pointed out: 'Some of my classmates have a private Instagram. I'm not allowed, but I watch them make stories sometimes.'

Communicating with teachers

Teacher interactions consistently popped up in Gen Alpha's comments. Many mentioned emailing or using a teacher-managed discussion board. A 12-year-old said: 'We have a class website. It's not fancy, but we can leave questions about homework. Our teacher replies to everyone the next day.' Others described teacher-run group chats. An 11-year-old explained: 'We used a teacher's WhatsApp group for a school trip, but she was in every conversation, so we had to be polite and not spam.'

Survey respondents said they want learning tools and class discussions to be interactive, fun and easy to use. They also hope teachers understand the value of quick feedback and personal guidance.

When it comes to well-integrated technology in schools, there was a mixed picture. Certain platforms are text heavy or slow to update, leaving kids dependent on teacher directions. An 11-year-old expressed frustration about mixed practices: 'One teacher uses an app with videos and fun quizzes. Another just hands out paper. I like the fun app, but only one class uses it, so I don't get to do it often.'

These stories highlight a generation learning digital etiquette at a younger age than previous generations. They must be aware of adult presence in most of their online spaces. This dynamic encourages them to blend respectful communication with the quick, informal styles typical of their peer interactions.

Striking a balance

What stands out across the survey is the balance that Generation Alphas strike between online and offline worlds. They are digital natives who often explore email, forums or collaboration apps. But they also demonstrate a strong preference for face-to-face connection, partly because they see it as more immediate and partly because they do not always have the means or freedom to go digital 24/7. Perhaps as parents and educators develop their understanding of technology, they are better placed to guide the next generation.

Plenty of Gen Alpha children expressed a healthy mix of curiosity and caution regarding technology. A ten-year-old said, 'I love playing an online game with my classmates, but if it's sunny, we'd rather go outside.' This statement captures a spirit of moderation. They dip into virtual worlds for fun or homework, but many remain just as keen on real-world adventures.

Patterns and implications

The survey data reveals some clear themes. Most Gen Alpha kids have partial or shared digital access, often regulated by adults. They prioritise in-person conversation for quick exchanges and use technology for homework tasks or keeping in touch with family. Those in more tech-forward schools mentioned collaboration tools, while others have a lot less access.

Looking ahead, these children are poised to rapidly become proficient in digital tools as they get older and parental restrictions ease, probably in their teenage years. They are likely to carry forward the respectful communication habits learned from teacher or parent oversight, blended with their innate understanding of online platforms. Yet it is also evident that they thrive on real-world interaction, cherishing the moments they can chat, play and learn away from screens.

What does Gen Alpha want from older generations?

Children at this stage appreciate that adults need to impose rules but want more involvement in understanding the 'why' behind them. They yearn for a bit of trust and opportunities to learn how to handle online communication responsibly, rather than blanket prohibitions. This could mean co-viewing apps with a parent or having short digital lessons in class that explain safe and respectful online behaviour.

Whether it's a teacher writing a smiley note on an assignment or a parent praising them for solving a problem, they crave clear affirmation. Digital communication, like sending a quick message or receiving a typed comment, can be exciting, but the personal touch of a conversation or handwritten note still resonates strongly for many in this age group. When it comes to schools' digital learning platforms, Gen Alpha craves simple menus and bright visuals, and immediate rewards or feedback loops go a long way. A ten-year-old commented: 'If the app is too boring or has too much writing, I lose interest. But if it's colourful and I can get stars or points, that makes me want to use it.'

Summing up Generation Alpha

Generation Alpha's voices reveal a group that is comfortable with technology without being fully immersed in it – yet. They embrace email and shared platforms when schools encourage them, and these children's natural openness to digital communication suggests they will probably adapt quickly once they reach an age when looser restrictions apply. Meanwhile, the pressure on parents to allow the use of digital devices like smartphones is growing and those asking are getting younger.

For those wanting to understand this generation, be it educators, parents or future employers, it's crucial to recognise their enthusiasm and constraints. Gen Alphas show an impressive aptitude for new tools and a love for traditional, in-person conversation. Their balance of offline and online approaches might just remind the rest of us that technology can be empowering when combined with the human touch. And if their survey comments are anything to go by, they plan on keeping that real-world connection firmly in place as they grow.

17 Generations at work 1 – the view from HR

When I started writing this book, I had the objective of helping my readers develop a greater understanding of each other so we can improve the way we live and work together. With a multigenerational workplace, it is important to understand how we all communicate across those generations. It's often said that the way we communicate at work can either build bridges or create silos. If you add different generations into the mix, those communication habits can become even more complex. In the previous chapter, I introduced what my Communication Habits and Preferences Survey 2024 found about Generation Alpha, who will start entering the workplace in 2030. The transition from Generation Z, half of whom were already in work in 2025, will be a gradual one. Understanding all of those starting their working lives, as well as those already in the workplace, is crucial.

When I commissioned my first survey, the Generations in the Workplace Study 2023, it was with the aim of seeing if there really was a generational problem in the workplace or not. I worked with research specialists Dynata to gather responses from 110 HR professionals across different industries and ask them about communication in their workplaces. I was keen to understand how different generations interact and what kinds of challenges or opportunities these interactions bring.

My main aim was to understand if there was any inter-generational friction and where communication was working and where it wasn't. The results offered illuminating insights into communication preferences, workplace conflicts, staff turnover and the ways in which HR teams are managing multi-generational employees. In this chapter, I'll reveal that first survey's key findings, focusing on challenges, staff turnover trends, anomalies in the data, patterns in communication preferences and what it all might mean for businesses of different sizes.

My hope is that by the end of this chapter, you'll come away with practical knowledge about how these insights can help build a more harmonious and productive work environment. Then compare these results with Chapter 18, where you'll hear how people saw themselves in the workplace, rather than the HR perspective.

Industry-specific insights

The survey of HR managers showed how generational dynamics played out differently across industries. In technology, for example, the fast pace of change highlighted the innovative contributions of younger employees but also underscored the challenge of retaining them in a competitive market. Those in the education and healthcare sectors emphasised the importance of intergenerational collaboration, with respondents frequently citing the benefits of combining the energy of youth with the experience of older staff.

Conversely, industries such as manufacturing and construction reported fewer generational challenges, likely due to more uniform workforces and clearer hierarchies. Retail and hospitality respondents noted the challenge of managing diverse teams and aligning expectations between younger and older employees.

The role of organisation size

The size of an organisation also played a significant role in shaping perceptions. Larger organisations were more likely to recognise the need for strategies to bridge generational gaps, often citing structured diversity and inclusion initiatives as part of their approach. One HR professional from a large organisation observed: 'We are looking to survey the population regarding benefits to see what's needed and will build a strategy from there.' In smaller organisations, generational differences were often seen as less significant. These workplaces tended to rely on direct communication and informal relationships, which may mitigate some generational tensions. However, the absence of formal policies could mean missed opportunities to fully leverage the strengths of a multigenerational workforce.

The HR view of younger generations

In the survey, younger employees, particularly Millennials and Gen Z, were viewed as ambitious, innovative and confident. Their ease with technology and openness to change were seen as key assets. Yet these same generations were often criticised for what some respondents perceived as entitlement, unrealistic salary expectations and a lack of resilience. One respondent highlighted the challenge succinctly: 'In the past five years, I find it very difficult to relate to some younger employees who expect salaries far in excess of what they should be earning, given their experience.'

This sentiment was not universal, however. Several HR professionals emphasised the immense value younger generations bring to the table, particularly their fresh perspectives and adaptability. Cross-generational mentorship, where younger employees bring technological expertise and older employees provide guidance and context, was cited as a significant opportunity.

The HR view of older generations

Older employees, particularly Baby Boomers and the Silent Generation, were described as reliable, experienced and dedicated. Their institutional knowledge and leadership skills were often celebrated. However, some respondents noted resistance to change and difficulties adapting to new technologies as recurring challenges.

Interestingly but probably unsurprisingly, older HR professionals were more likely to express concerns about the work ethic and loyalty of younger generations. Conversely, younger HR professionals showed greater empathy toward their peers, focusing on their potential and the need to modernise workplace practices to better align with younger workers' expectations.

HR challenges with different generations

One of the survey's central questions asked: 'What is the biggest HR challenge you face when dealing with different generations in your workforce?' The answers varied, but a few common themes did emerge.

The most significant for me was that 68 per cent of respondents indicated that 'differing communication preferences' was their top challenge. This ranged from the method of communication, such as emails versus face-to-face conversations versus instant messaging, to the tone and style of communication. Generationally, this is what it looked like:

- **Baby Boomers:** Many noted that Baby Boomers often prefer in-person conversations or phone calls. They appreciate the time taken to talk through details and often find email to be a more official record of communication rather than their primary method for hashing out an idea.

- **Generation X:** This group, while comfortable with email and phone, is said to be highly adaptable. Many Gen X employees embrace email as a default but are also open to Slack or Teams messages when the situation calls for quick back and forth.

- **Millennials:** This generation generally uses a variety of communication tools, but the survey indicated that Millennials lean toward quick, efficient messaging platforms. They also tend to like visual platforms such as embedded videos, or chats with emojis, and appreciate feedback delivered in near-real time.

- **Generation Z:** The youngest cohort in the workforce has grown up with smartphones and social media. They're often more comfortable with short, frequent bursts of communication. According to several HR managers, Gen Z employees sometimes show reluctance towards long emails, finding them 'old school' or unnecessarily formal.

This variety of communication styles and preferences presents an ongoing challenge. HR teams need to create guidelines that respect each generation's comfort level while encouraging everyone to meet in the middle.

Varying expectations on feedback and recognition

Another common challenge HR managers pointed out was the difference in how each generation views feedback and recognition. According to 54 per cent of the HR respondents, older generations sometimes feel that giving praise 'too often' is annoying and unnecessary, while younger employees thrive on regular acknowledgement.

- **Frequent feedback:** Millennials and Gen Zers were described as wanting more frequent check-ins – monthly, if not weekly. They seek quick, constructive critiques and appreciate regular praise for a job well done, even if it's minor.

- **Structured feedback:** Baby Boomers and Gen Xers generally expect formal performance reviews once or twice a year, though they do not mind occasional one-on-one chats. Many HR professionals noted that these employees still value recognition but don't necessarily need it weekly.

Conflict point: Some Baby Boomers and Gen X employees can interpret the need for frequent feedback as a lack of independence, while Millennials and Gen Zers sometimes feel neglected if there isn't ongoing dialogue.

Attitudes toward hierarchy and authority

When HR professionals were asked about management and leadership style preferences, nearly half (48 per cent) observed friction stemming from generational attitudes towards hierarchy.

Traditional hierarchies: Baby Boomers and, to a lesser extent, some Gen X employees were described as more comfortable with a clear chain of command. They respect authority that is tied to tenure and expertise.

Flattened structures: Millennials and Gen Z, on the other hand, often prefer a more relaxed, team-based approach. They don't necessarily believe in blindly following orders based solely on someone's seniority. Instead, they want a justification of why a process or policy is in place and don't mind challenging the status quo to find more efficient solutions – especially younger Gen Zers. This can create tension when managers from older generations perceive questioning as a lack of respect, while younger employees see it as simply contributing ideas. Several respondents said that clarifying the 'why' behind decisions has helped bridge this gap.

The connection between staff turnover, company size and generational factors

Another area that the survey explored was the relationship between staff turnover and both the size of the company and the generations most likely to leave. The results shed light on several key points. Around 40 per cent of HR professionals from companies with fewer than 100 employees mentioned higher turnover rates among Millennials and Gen Z staff. This finding was partly attributed to:

- **Limited career growth:** Smaller organisations often have fewer internal pathways for promotion. Younger employees, who might crave rapid career development, are more likely to jump ship if there's no clear ladder to climb.

- **Burnout:** In a small company, employees sometimes wear multiple hats. Some younger staff reported to their HR bosses that they feel the extra load leads to quick burnout, especially if they perceive that their additional contributions aren't rewarded with faster promotions or regular pay raises.

Conversely, in organisations with more than 1,000 employees, HR professionals noted that turnover tended to spike more among Generation X and Baby Boomers at mid-career or pre-retirement stages. They suggested the reasons for this included:

- **Feeling stagnant:** Some mid-career professionals felt overlooked in huge corporate structures, especially if promotions seemed to favour younger, tech-savvy colleagues.

- **Restructuring stress:** Large corporations often have reorganisations, mergers or frequent departmental changes. These shifts can create uncertainty, particularly for Baby Boomers who, according to the survey responses, prefer job security in the later phases of their careers.

Interestingly, respondents across the board reported that Gen Z tends to be highly mobile, regardless of company size. More than 60 per cent of HR professionals noted that Gen Z employees are likely to explore new opportunities if they aren't quickly engaged and challenged. On the flip side, if a workplace offers continuous learning and a sense of purpose, Gen Z might remain loyal even in a small firm.

Many HR professionals remarked that younger employees often say 'poor communication' is a primary reason for leaving an organisation. This includes:

- lack of transparent updates about company direction

- insufficient, infrequent or overly formal feedback

- limited collaborative platforms (such as Slack, Teams or project management software).

Meanwhile, older employees left companies where they felt their experience and input were no longer valued or recognised, which can also be tied to communication styles. For instance, if leadership rarely consults senior staff about policy changes, Baby Boomers may feel marginalised.

Generational communication preferences and behaviour through an HR lens

The heart of the survey dealt with the specifics of 'how' each generation prefers to communicate on a daily basis and in formal settings, such as performance reviews. It's interesting to see how closely the results of the survey of HR professionals correlates with the responses in the Communication Habits and Preferences Survey 2024 discussed in Chapter 13.

On a daily basis, this is how, according to the HR professionals who took part in the 2023 survey, different generations like to communicate:

- **Baby Boomers:** Phone calls and in-person meetings remain popular. Many Baby Boomers indicated comfort with email, but they prefer it for more formal exchanges.

- **Generation X:** Flexible in using phone, email and messaging apps. They often adapt to whichever platform is standard in the company, but about 45 per cent prefer email if they have to share detailed information.

- **Millennials:** Tend to default to email for asynchronous communication but love quick messaging platforms for immediate feedback or brainstorming. Some 35 per cent of HR professionals said their Millennial employees feel stifled without group chats.

✦ **Generation Z:** Leans heavily on real-time digital communication – instant messages, video calls and even voice notes. A small subset (about 10 per cent) also expressed a preference for short video or voice messages over typed text.

When it comes to formal communications like performance reviews, older generations prefer scheduled, structured conversations in annual or semi-annual reviews. Younger generations want real-time or monthly feedback. If the communication centres around conflict resolution, Generation X and Baby Boomers are more likely to want a face-to-face conversation for serious issues, while Millennials and Gen Zers are more open to an initial resolution chat via video call or a shared online workspace. However, it was noted that all generations ultimately appreciate face-to-face or at least video communication for finalising solutions to major conflicts. For team meetings, Baby Boomers and Gen X see in-person group meetings as valuable for building rapport, while Millennials and Gen Z, though open to in-person meets, often stress the need for digital follow-ups such as shared meeting notes in the cloud or a quick Slack recap.

Tools and technologies

About 64 per cent of HR professionals said they've had to roll out or refine their messaging platforms and project management tools to accommodate the wide range of preferences. The tools mentioned were:

✦ **Slack/Teams:** Favoured by Millennials and Gen Z for daily communications.

✦ **Emails:** Still essential for official communications; often more comfortable for Baby Boomers and Gen X.

✦ **Project management software:** Tools such as Trello, Monday.com or Asana appealed across generations – once adequate training was provided.

෴ **Corporate social networks:** A small slice of HR professionals (around 5 per cent) reported using social media-like platforms (such as Yammer) to encourage knowledge sharing and a sense of community.

Patterns and common themes

In my research, I always look for patterns that can guide us to what's happening generationally in the workplace. A recurring theme across responses was the importance of effective communication. Respondents highlighted that bridging generational differences requires not just understanding but active listening and open dialogue. As one participant aptly put it: 'The best thing anyone in this situation can do is just keep an open mind and listen. Both generations can learn from the other.'

Many HR professionals also emphasised that generational labels, while useful, can sometimes overshadow other important factors such as cultural background, personality and individual experiences. One respondent noted: 'To focus purely on age as a key determinant is a mistake. Backgrounds, cultures and styles are equally, if not more, influential than age.'

There will never be absolute answers to bridge the generation gaps but when the same topics keep coming up it's worth noting them. The first was the recognition of how important the onboarding process is and then how effective the training is afterwards. Regardless of their generation, employees across the board perform better when they are given thorough onboarding and continuous training. Many HR professionals (more than 70 per cent) agreed that investing in learning tools that accommodate multiple learning styles (videos, written manuals, interactive sessions) can ease generational friction. Younger staff benefit from tech-based training modules, while older staff often appreciate in-person workshops for more nuanced discussions.

Another major theme that seemed to cross generational divides was the universal desire for respect and inclusion. Whether you're 25 or 65, being heard and valued is essential. HR teams who foster an inclusive culture, where every voice counts and people are encouraged to contribute ideas, reported fewer instances of tension between generational cohorts.

Flexibility is a word that frequently emerges as something employees are looking for at work, although how each person defines it may differ. This includes looking for flexible working hours, flexible communication styles and flexible approaches to hierarchy where expertise is recognised over age or title. These all came up repeatedly as ways to keep employees engaged, regardless of which generation they belong to.

The survey also underscored that leadership sets the tone. If the leadership team uses open, multichannel communication, employees are more likely to follow suit. This means using email, chat and face-to-face meetings effectively and together rather than focusing on just one. If the leadership leans heavily on just one mode of communication (for example, all communication is done via mass email), the rest of the workforce may feel compelled to stick to that style whether they like it or not. This can frustrate those who might prefer different methods, especially among the younger cohort.

Anomalies in the survey

Many of the survey results painted a picture you might expect – such as Baby Boomers preferring more traditional modes of communication while Gen Z is all about quick messages. However, there were some anomalies worth noting, which also appeared in the 2024 survey into communication preferences.

Around 8 per cent of HR managers noted that some of their Baby Boomer employees are more tech-savvy than you might have thought and some more than their younger counterparts. These older employees are often enthusiastic about new software and frequently early adopters if they see the practical benefits. Meanwhile, a subset of Millennials resisted learning new tools, citing 'software fatigue' or feeling overwhelmed by too many apps. This contradiction highlights that while generational categories can suggest patterns, they're not absolute rules.

Another anomaly emerged regarding feedback. Although common narratives suggest that younger employees crave constant praise, 12 per cent of HR professionals described experiences with Gen Z staff who prefer straightforward, even critical feedback. It appears these employees resent 'sugar-coated' communication and want managers to be brutally honest so they can improve quickly. Having said that, many younger employees were perceived as less accustomed to constructive feedback, a gap some respondents attributed to educational systems.

Finally, a small but significant group of HR professionals observed that generational differences can lead to a productive 'reverse mentorship'. For example, a Gen Z employee might guide a Baby Boomer on social media marketing strategies, while the Baby Boomer imparts wisdom about client relations and industry history. This synergy is not necessarily an anomaly, but it was described as an unexpected benefit rather than the norm. It's also worth noting that some assume friction is the only outcome of mixing generations.

Conclusions from my workplace survey

When you step back and look at the complete picture painted by this survey of HR professionals, one thing stands out: diverse generational workforces have immense potential for synergy. Yes, there are clear differences in communication preferences, attitudes toward feedback, comfort with hierarchy and loyalty patterns. However, with intentional strategies and an open-minded approach, these potential friction points can be transformed into opportunities for growth.

The survey findings highlighted the misconceptions about work ethic, loyalty and adaptability that persist and sometimes create unnecessary friction. It seems that smaller organisations often lack the resources or frameworks to address generational differences effectively. In Chapter 20, 'Thriving in a multigenerational workplace', I'll look in more detail at how management, supervisors and staff can use this research in their workplaces and create more generationally cohesive work environments.

This perspective from HR managers was a fascinating glimpse into what's happening in the workplace today. In many ways, these findings reaffirm that communication is at the core of any organisation's success. By understanding the general tendencies of different generations and then taking the time to get to know each employee's individual preferences, companies can reduce staff turnover, improve job satisfaction and create a more cohesive environment.

The real takeaway from this survey is that generational differences don't have to be stumbling blocks: they can be stepping stones towards a more dynamic and cohesive workplace culture.

18 Generations at work 2 – what those at work are seeing

The workplace currently has four generations on its payroll and if you include the relatively few people working past the age of 79, then that would make five. While there are no official statistics for those over 80 years old still working, the UK's Office for National Statistics reported that approximately 1.468 million individuals aged 65 and over were employed as of April to June 2022, representing 11 per cent of their age group.

In my Communication Habits and Preferences Survey 2024, 2,047 of the sample over the age of 18 were working at the time they responded, while a further 134 had been in paid work in the previous 12 months. Of the total 2,181 people in employment, 40 per cent mainly worked in an office environment and 23 per cent at home. Others worked in a range of settings, including retail stores, warehouses, factories, hospitals and schools. Among the sample, 39 per cent of workers said they manage other people.

When it comes to the different generations at work, this is a constantly moving picture. Just 2 per cent of working respondents were from the Silent Generation, followed by 15 per cent Baby Boomers, 20 per cent Gen Zers (18 to 27) and 28 per cent Gen Xers, with Gen Y (Millennials) the largest generation represented at 35 per cent. It would be reasonable to expect the largest generation in the workforce to have the greatest influence on modern workplace practices. Bear in mind that Millennials are often mid-career professionals, team leaders or newly minted senior managers. They grew up alongside the digital revolution, typically comfortable with multiple communication platforms but also mindful of work–life balance.

In this chapter, I will explore how my survey sheds light on how individuals in each generation approach workplace communication, from the tools they prefer to the tone they use, all the way to the kind of feedback they value most. This is an illuminating comparison to the results of the Generations in the Workplace 2023 survey I wrote about in the last chapter, which looked at these issues from an HR perspective. This chapter looks at why different age groups communicate in the ways they do, and where these habits occasionally break the stereotypical perception of their generation or create unexpected overlaps.

Working from home or going into work?

Hardly a day goes past when there isn't a debate about working from home (often referred to as WFH) versus getting people back to their places of work – although clearly this isn't always a choice for many people in certain industries who responded to the survey. The survey showed that around half of those in work were either based at home or at least spent some time working from home. However, the figures were lower for 18 to 21-year-olds, with only 34 per cent having spent any time working from home.

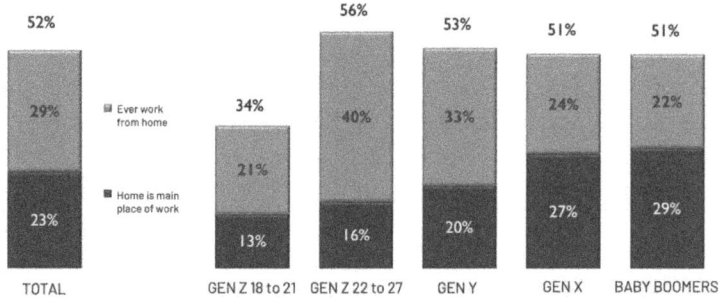

Communication Habits and Preferences Survey 2024: Do respondents work from home

The really fascinating data emerged when those who mainly or ever worked at home were asked: 'When you're working, where do you feel more productive?' There was quite a generational split, with 55 per cent of 22 to 27-year-olds feeling more productive at work compared with just 22 per cent of Baby Boomers. However, it's interesting to see that 55 per cent of Boomers felt they work equally effectively at home or at work – the highest of any generation. It's also noteworthy that younger Gen Zers (18 to 21) feel more productive working from home (45 per cent) but for older members of the same generation (22 to 27) that almost halves to 23 per cent.

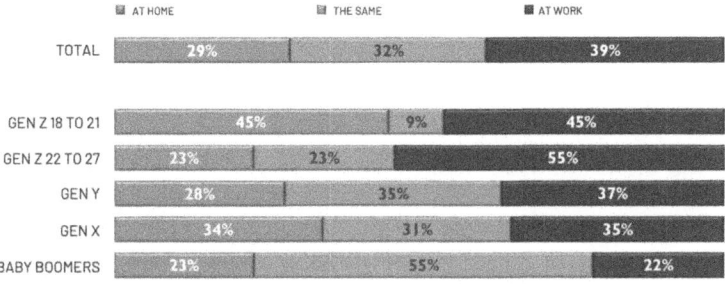

Communication Habits and Preferences Survey 2024: Where do respondents feel more productive

Networking

When asked if their job ever involved networking in person, the generation who reported networking the most was the older Gen Z group at 61 per cent, followed by Gen Y (Millennials) at 51 per cent. All the other age groups were about the same at around 39 per cent. However, the really telling statistic is in the attitudes of the different generations towards networking in person.

Among the whole of Gen Z, 23 per cent will only network if they are told to, while 32 per cent of 22 to 27-year-olds say they prefer to do their networking online or in another way compared to in person. Older generations who are more experienced were less reluctant, but still only 44 per cent of Baby Boomers reported quite liking the in-person networking experience.

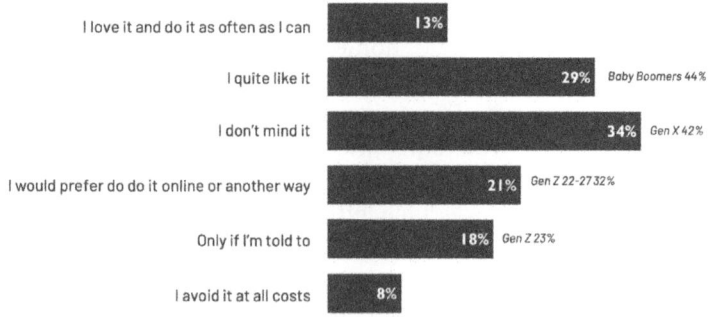

I love it and do it as often as I can — 13%

I quite like it — 29% Baby Boomers 44%

I don't mind it — 34% Gen X 42%

I would prefer do do it online or another way — 21% Gen Z 22-27 32%

Only if I'm told to — 18% Gen Z 23%

I avoid it at all costs — 8%

Communication Habits and Preferences Survey 2024: How respondents prefer to network

Internal communication

The phone and email continue to dominate workplace communication. Older age groups in particular emphasised that they value the personal touch and clarity of real-time voice interaction. Although email was popular, several Gen X and Boomer respondents did mention that email chains can quickly become cumbersome, especially if they were trying to gauge the tone of a message or resolve a delicate matter. 'You can't hear a smile in an email,' one Baby Boomer observed. Another comment revealed a Silent Generation participant still cherishing 'the sound of a friendly voice' as it leaves less room for misunderstanding and fosters a greater sense of connection.

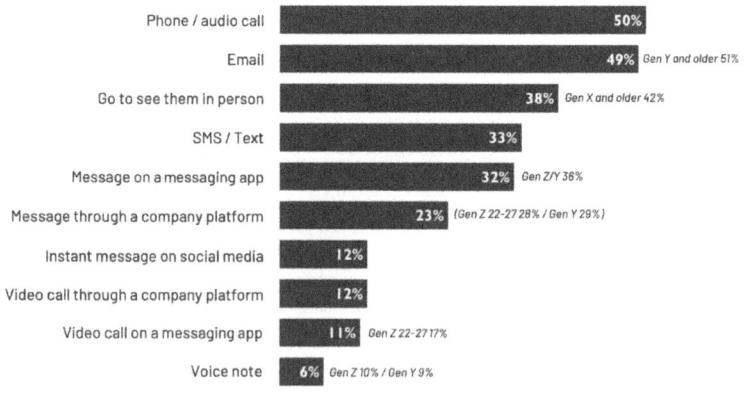

Phone / audio call — 50%

Email — 49% Gen Y and older 51%

Go to see them in person — 38% Gen X and older 42%

SMS / Text — 33%

Message on a messaging app — 32% Gen Z/Y 38%

Message through a company platform — 23% (Gen Z 22-27 28% / Gen Y 29%)

Instant message on social media — 12%

Video call through a company platform — 12%

Video call on a messaging app — 11% Gen Z 22-27 17%

Voice note — 6% Gen Z 10% / Gen Y 9%

Communication Habits and Preferences Survey 2024: Preferred work contact methods for respondents

It's the younger generations (Y and Z) who are keen on instant messaging platforms such as Slack or Microsoft Teams. This preference for real-time digital conversation in the workplace over more formal or asynchronous means was not exclusive to the younger groups, though. An interesting subset of Gen X respondents (aged 44 to 59) also indicated that they feel more comfortable using instant messaging for quick updates as they find it less intrusive than a phone call yet more immediate than email. One Gen X respondent even remarked: 'I like the idea of dropping someone a quick ping. It's not as formal as an email, which can feel like it needs a salutation and a signature. But it doesn't demand the immediate attention of a phone call.' This comment illustrates a key trend highlighted in the data: while younger generations may be drawn to chat-based platforms, older generations appreciate these tools for their efficiency.

Although video calls on platforms such as Teams, Zoom and Google Meet did take place before 2020, it was the pandemic that accelerated the move to online communication. Now more than 55 per cent communicate by video call, with Gen Y (Millennials) being the most prolific online (63 per cent). The difference lies in how each generation chooses to take that virtual call. While a Gen Z team member might feel no qualms about quickly accepting a video call on a mobile device while walking through the corridor, a Gen X participant may still prefer to use a laptop to connect. One Millennial respondent remarked: 'I carry my phone everywhere – I can jump on a quick Zoom or Teams call without having to power up a computer, which is great if I'm in transit or between different work sites.'

That said, many older respondents in the survey displayed an unexpected adaptability, contrasting with the stereotype that older generations are tech averse. In fact it is Baby Boomers who like communicating by video call the most, at 40 per cent.

Boomers have willingly embraced video calls for client meetings, mentorship discussions and day-to-day check-ins with colleagues. While younger generations may have a certain fluency with these tools from the start, many older professionals have shown an enthusiasm for the technology once they receive adequate training and see its benefits. One Silent Generation respondent commented: 'I started using Zoom during the pandemic and discovered it's a lot easier than I expected. I still like meeting face to face, but this is convenient.'

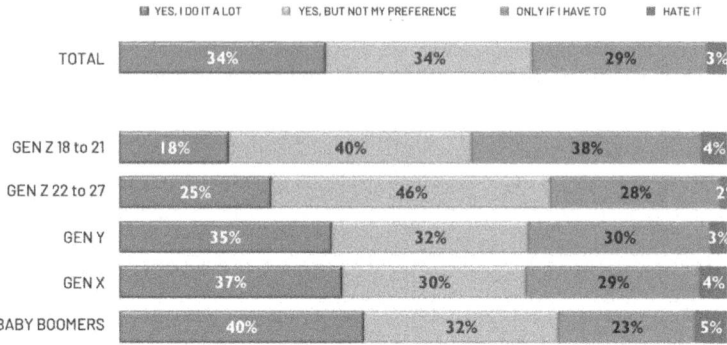

Communication Habits and Preferences Survey 2024: Do respondents like using video calling at work?

One thing that did come up was the feeling of overwhelm caused by the multiplicity of communication platforms used in the workplace of today – especially in older generations. One Baby Boomer respondent shared a sentiment that came up multiple times: 'I learned email when it replaced memos, then I tackled instant messages, and now I'm asked to be on half a dozen different apps. I do it, but it's exhausting.' In many ways, this is not about a lack of capability; rather, it is about a pace of change that can feel relentless in modern work settings.

Dealing with people at work

To explore how respondents felt about working with others, the survey offered a range of scenarios to gauge their reaction and see how this varied generationally, including preferences on independent working, levels of ambition and formality of both procedures and interactions with colleagues.

While one might expect younger generations to be ambitious to move up in their career, as borne out by the figures in the table above, that Gen Xers were evenly split in their ambitions is more of a surprise. Many of the generational differences come from the level of experience in the workplace and are also a reflection of new generations coming in and pushing for new styles of working. This is perfectly illustrated when it came to different generations' preference for a more formal or informal tone when interacting with colleagues and superiors, where the results painted a nuanced picture.

I prefer to work by myself

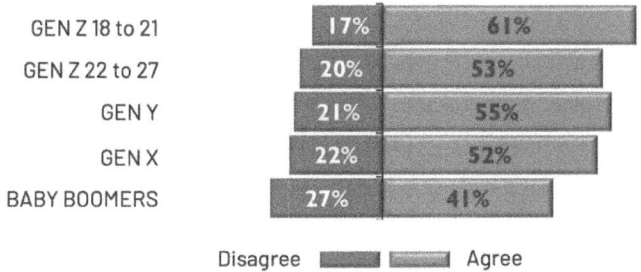

I'm ambitious to move up in my career

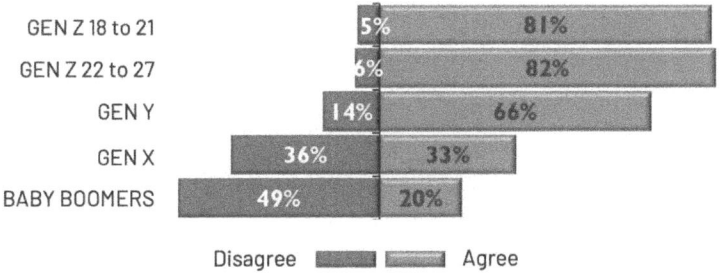

Communication Habits and Preferences Survey 2024: Respondents' attitudes to working with others 1

A majority of Generation X respondents, for instance, indicated they prefer a middle ground: starting off respectfully and somewhat formally, particularly if they are conversing with senior management, but then shifting to a more relaxed tone as the relationship develops. Conversely, a considerable proportion of Gen Zers and Millennials favoured a more casual style from the outset, tending to use more friendly greetings or humorous sign-offs even in their first interactions. The Silent Generation and Baby Boomers often view formality as a sign of respect and good manners. 'A short greeting and a proper sign-off show that you take the other person seriously,' one Silent Generation respondent noted. These generational norms around how to write or speak in a professional context are often shaped by formative work experiences, which can differ substantially depending on the era in which someone began their career.

I believe that formal procedures and policies restrict people

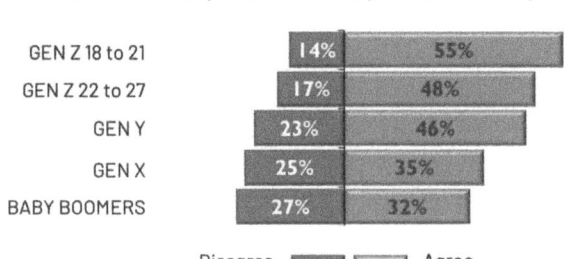

I tend to have distant, rather formal, relationships with people at work

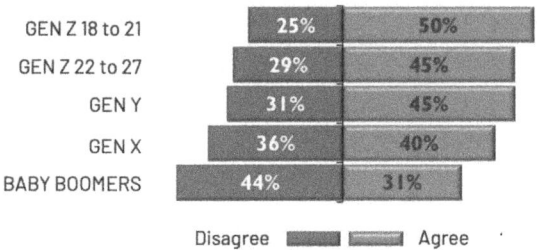

Communication Habits and Preferences Survey 2024: Respondents' attitudes to working with others 2

Feedback in the workplace

A key feature in the workplace is the level of feedback that employees want versus the amount they actually receive. Just like the students at school and university, discussed in Chapter 15, there is a disparity between expectation and reality, while it's also interesting to compare the desire for feedback from the perspective of HR managers in the previous chapter. You'll see there is a lot of consistency between them all.

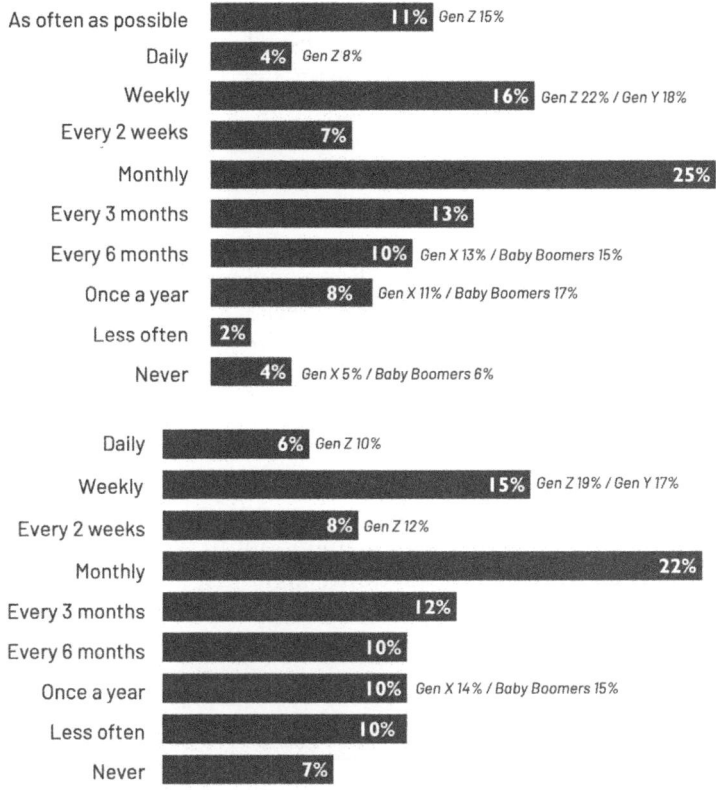

As often as possible	**11%**	Gen Z 15%
Daily	**4%**	Gen Z 8%
Weekly	**16%**	Gen Z 22% / Gen Y 18%
Every 2 weeks	**7%**	
Monthly	**25%**	
Every 3 months	**13%**	
Every 6 months	**10%**	Gen X 13% / Baby Boomers 15%
Once a year	**8%**	Gen X 11% / Baby Boomers 17%
Less often	**2%**	
Never	**4%**	Gen X 5% / Baby Boomers 6%

Daily	**6%**	Gen Z 10%
Weekly	**15%**	Gen Z 19% / Gen Y 17%
Every 2 weeks	**8%**	Gen Z 12%
Monthly	**22%**	
Every 3 months	**12%**	
Every 6 months	**10%**	
Once a year	**10%**	Gen X 14% / Baby Boomers 15%
Less often	**10%**	
Never	**7%**	

Communication Habits and Preferences Survey 2024: Feedback preferences (preferred, top, and actual)

My survey supports the research from Northumbria and Edinburgh Napier universities (Grant et al 2021), which suggests that Generation Z employees 'prefer feedback' and value mentoring, and a *Forbes* article (Arturi 2024) that noted Millennials 'crave frequent feedback' and thrive in collaborative environments. While the survey showed that 41 per cent are getting feedback less often than they would like (Gen Z and Gen Y), it appears that 19 per cent (mainly Gen X and Boomers) are actually getting more frequent feedback than they would like. This would suggest that organisations are recognising that the younger generations want more feedback but are treating all employees the same rather than recognising their different needs. This survey highlights the challenges with a one-size-fits-all strategy.

The results showed that across all generations, in-person or voice-based feedback is generally considered more meaningful and less prone to misunderstanding than written forms, especially when it pertains to performance reviews or major project critiques. Yet there was an interesting twist: Gen Z respondents indicated they are equally comfortable receiving structured feedback via messaging apps, provided it is timely and well-organised. A Gen Z participant wrote, 'As long as I know what I did right, what I did wrong, and how to improve, the method of delivery isn't a big deal – just let me know as soon as possible.' This flexible approach stands in contrast to the preference of some Baby Boomers who felt that certain topics, such as performance evaluations, should be discussed face to face for the sake of clarity and respect. Another Gen X respondent summarised their attitude to feedback with the comment: 'We don't want to turn everything into a meeting, but some conversations are too important to be left to text, no matter how advanced the platform might be.'

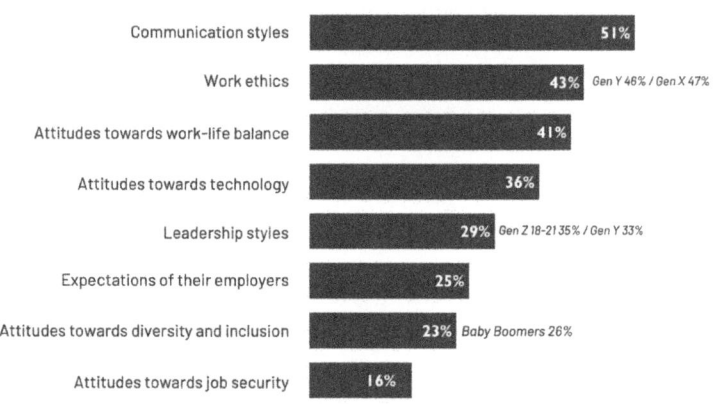

Communication styles	51%
Work ethics	43% Gen Y 46% / Gen X 47%
Attitudes towards work-life balance	41%
Attitudes towards technology	36%
Leadership styles	29% Gen Z 18-21 35% / Gen Y 33%
Expectations of their employers	25%
Attitudes towards diversity and inclusion	23% Baby Boomers 26%
Attitudes towards job security	16%

Communication Habits and Preferences Survey 2024: Respondents' view of how the way people think and behave varies, depending on their age

Summing up the feeling of many respondents was this salient quote from a Gen Y (Millennial) manager, who commented: 'We're a team of Baby Boomers, Gen X and Millennials, and while we definitely have our pet peeves – like reading five-paragraph emails when a one-liner would do – we mostly learn from each other. I've shown my older colleagues shortcuts in Slack, while they've taught me how to write a concise, polite email. We get on well, honestly.'

A Baby Boomer interviewee commented: 'I started my working life with memos typed on a typewriter, and now I'm sending animated GIFs in Teams. It's been a journey, and I'm actually proud I've kept up.'

What stands out across these findings is that generational differences are real, but they are not monolithic. Yes, young people may be quicker to pick up new tools and older people might prefer time-tested methods, but the lines blur in practice. Many respondents, particularly in Gen X, seem to straddle the gap, adapting to both older and newer communication channels. Meanwhile, many Baby Boomers are learning eagerly from younger colleagues when the benefits of a new approach are clear, and Gen Z can be surprisingly traditional about certain aspects of communication etiquette. The survey has shown that there are pockets of overlap, anomalies and plenty of comments from people who defy the stereotype, like the 79-year-old management consultant who said: 'I never expected to still be working at my age, but technology helps me contribute. I do worry about being left behind on the latest platforms, though.'

Expectations for the future workplace

Based on the survey's open-ended responses, many participants anticipate further evolutions in workplace communication, with many hoping companies consolidate communication tools to reduce duplication and confusion. A 38-year-old Millennial manager predicted: 'In five years, we'll see simpler, integrated systems. Slack, email, Teams – maybe there'll be one universal hub.'

Hybrid or remote models of working seem poised to remain, but organisations will need to refine policies to prevent burnout and ensure meaningful collaboration. A 25-year-old Gen Z employee said: 'If a company tries to revert to 100 per cent on site, they risk losing younger talent.' I'll talk more about this in Chapter 20, 'Thriving in a multigenerational workforce'. Technology will certainly have a big role in the future workplace, as BBC technology correspondent Paul Carter told me on my podcast: 'Automation, AI and robotics will drive the biggest workplace changes for future generations.'

My survey supported what is reported almost daily in the media: that demands for mental wellbeing, inclusive communication and flexible scheduling are likely to intensify. Far from giving up on technology, Baby Boomers and Silent Generation participants are looking to advanced tech features such as auto transcription or larger, simplified interfaces to help them stay engaged in the workplace for longer.

Finally, many respondents see the potential in formalising mentorship. Younger staff could teach digital shortcuts; older staff could share institutional wisdom. 'If we structure it well, it's a win–win,' noted a 45-year-old Gen X HR director. Again, I'll come back to this in Chapter 20, which looks at some of the best practices that successful organisations are adopting to create more generationally cohesive workplaces.

Summing up the generations at work

While clear, age-based trends do exist, there are numerous exceptions and overlapping preferences that defy simple stereotypes. These findings underline the reality that successful communication at work rarely stems from the blanket adoption of the newest tools or from clinging to older, more familiar methods. Instead, it is about integrating the best practices from every generation, choosing the channel that suits the task at hand and showing respect for others' comfort zones. While many respondents felt frustrated with their workplaces, it was good to read how often some respondents mentioned learning and growth as well as mutual mentoring where two individuals, typically from different ages, backgrounds, experience levels or perspectives, engage in a two-way exchange of knowledge, support and guidance. This to me is evidence that intergenerational teams can adapt together to the changing demands of the modern workplace.

Whether it's a quick Slack message to confirm a meeting, a thoughtful phone call to ensure someone's wellbeing or a formal email to detail important project updates, the story is the same: communication is always a two-way street. Age might influence the turn we take, but it's not the final determinant of our destination. Companies that recognise and celebrate this diversity in communication styles create a dynamic space where each person, regardless of their generation, feels heard and empowered to share.

Every age group has room to adapt, learn and refine the art of communication for a workplace setting that keeps evolving. If you take anything from these survey findings, it should be that generational differences, while intriguing, are best viewed as points of shared learning.

19 Patterns or stereotypes?

I began looking at generational communication based on how we connect with each other and whether we are speaking the same language. As you will know by now, my mantra has always been that we are *framed* by our generation rather than *defined* by it. In other words, we do carry some typical generational traits, but we are far from carbon copies.

When I first set out on this study, I wanted to see whether I could put a finger on a precise figure to show just how stereotypical each generation truly is. Think of it like Douglas Adams' *The Hitchhiker's Guide to the Galaxy*, where the answer to the Ultimate Question is famously '42'. That answer was calculated by a supercomputer named Deep Thought over 7.5 million years. I've used AI to help me through our data set of 4,067 and to discover how closely each generation's communication behaviour aligns with their generational stereotype – and crucially, where it doesn't.

To do this, I asked AI the same closed questions that Dynata had asked the survey respondents, but based on the accepted views of each generation. I used two different platforms to get a more robust set of responses. I teamed up with Mark Mooji from Inqqa AI, who specialise in connecting the dots in employee research. Their core expertise lies in finding the insights you can get from open-ended feedback, because it allows the respondents to open their minds. While Mark looked at the opened-ended questions in my survey, for this exercise we focused on the closed questions to test how closely people matched generational assumptions.

What are generational stereotypes?

These are broad, culturally accepted assumptions about how people in each generation behave. In Section 2, I explored the background and typical traits often portrayed in the media or popular books. For the purposes of my comparison between the stereotypes and what my surveys revealed, Mark and I focused on communication style, technology, methods of communication, social media use and attitudes in the workplace. The stereotypical traits in these areas could be summarised as follows.

- **Silent Generation** (1928–1945): Often portrayed as reluctant to adopt newer technologies, strongly preferring phone calls or face-to-face interaction.

- **Baby Boomers** (1946–1964): Slightly more open to technology than Silent Gen but still rely heavily on phone calls and email. Sceptical of newer platforms like social media; prefer personal conversations or email for formal tasks.

- **Gen X** (1965–1980): Pragmatic 'bridge' generation that adopted digital tools in adulthood; comfortable with email, texting, phone calls; blends older and newer methods.

- **Millennials (Gen Y)** (1981–1996): Often seen as highly tech savvy; reliant on texting, social media, collaborative apps; comfortable blending personal and professional digital tools.

- **Gen Z** (1997–2011): 'Digital natives' frequently on social apps; prefer short-form content, quick messaging and real-time feedback; less likely to use phone calls or long emails.

- **Gen Alpha** (2012–2024): Young children under strict parental oversight, but already immersed in playful, gamified apps; gleaning early digital habits from older siblings or parents.

Communicate more through supervised platforms and face to face at school.

So, how did the real responses compare to these stereotypes?

Technology usage

✝ **Silent Gen:** The stereotype as the generation who rarely uses smartphones holds up well. They rely on landlines and have minimal interest in new apps. The survey revealed that about 70–75 per cent do lean heavily on phone calls and face to face. However, at 25 per cent, more than expected are video calling and using tablets.

✝ **Baby Boomers:** They broadly matched expectations as a generation mainly comfortable with email or phone. Although they are less comfortable with social media, many do use Facebook or WhatsApp to connect with family. However, a higher proportion than the stereotype suggests are tech savvy.

✝ **Gen X:** About half fit the pragmatic stereotype. The rest split between embracing new tech and sticking with old habits. Interestingly, some older Gen Xers in the survey reported not using smartphones as often as younger Gen Xers, hinting at splits within the generation.

✝ **Millennials (Gen Y):** Often labelled tech savvy – and broadly they are. But 45 per cent in my survey reported concerns about data and digital overload, suggesting they're more selective than the stereotype implies.

✝ **Gen Z:** It's said Gen Zers are inseparable from their smartphones and indeed this is the case, with 98 per cent owning one. As expected, they rarely make phone calls or email, but between 30 and 40 per cent said they appreciate phone calls or digital detox strategies, complicating the notion that they're always online.

✝ **Gen Alpha:** While 60 per cent of Gen Alphas use tablets, many still rely on face to face at school. Parental restrictions mean their digital freedom isn't as extensive as the stereotype suggests.

Methods of communication

- **Silent Gen:** As expected, 70 to 75 per cent do indeed rely primarily on calls and face to face. However, contrary to what we may assume, 61 per cent of them use WhatsApp – especially if grandchildren or younger colleagues encourage it.

- **Baby Boomers:** This generation stereotypically prefers calls and emails, and the survey generally supported this, with about 65 per cent relying on these methods on a daily basis.

- **Gen X:** Again, Gen Xers form the bridge, with half splitting their communication across texts, calls and email. The survey showed about half indeed bridging older and newer styles of communication.

- **Millennials (Gen Y):** Recognised for texting, group chats and email for more formal tasks – and we found around 55 to 60 per cent do have this blend of communication styles. In my survey, Millennials aligned more closely with Gen Z than Gen X in their dislike of phone calls or preference for shorter calls. This unexpected finding highlights 'Millennials' as a label can span a wide range of adult ages.

- **Gen Z:** They are known for short messages and group chats, and that's true for about half of them, but 32 per cent still pick up the phone to talk, which is more than the stereotype predicts.

- **Gen Alpha:** Because of their age (8 to 12 in my survey), Gen Alphas are almost forced into mostly face-to-face or parent-mediated device use. Roughly 40 per cent matched that pattern, with some use of supervised text and voice notes, while others relied heavily on in-person communication.

Social media usage

ᚦᚦᚦ **Silent Gen:** The expectation here is that this generation has minimal social media activity. My survey data showed that although 68 per cent rarely post, 32 per cent are active on social media, which is most often Facebook.

ᚦᚦᚦ **Baby Boomers:** These are often seen as a 'Facebook generation' who do not widely adopt other and new platforms. About 65 per cent are indeed mostly on Facebook or WhatsApp, with only 13 per cent exploring Instagram and even fewer on TikTok.

ᚦᚦᚦ **Gen X:** I've often referred to Gen Xers as the bridging generation as they enjoy a blend of older platforms like Facebook but also like the occasional use of Instagram or X. LinkedIn is popular with this generation, with about 50 per cent following the 'moderate but not overboard' pattern.

ᚦᚦᚦ **Millennials (Gen Y):** This generation typically posted heavily in their twenties and now they might use more private groups, with about 55 per cent matching the 'active on multiple platforms' stereotype.

ᚦᚦᚦ **Gen Z:** They have been stereotyped as heavily reliant on TikTok, Instagram and Snapchat. The data shows that actually 45 per cent are extremely active in short-form content, but many are cautious or prefer smaller private circles for their social media interaction.

ᚦᚦᚦ **Gen Alpha:** The stereotype for this generation (especially the survey's sample of 8 to 12-year-olds) is that they are on a constant stream of social media interaction, but actually about 60 per cent are restricted. Only 40 per cent show frequent or 'constant' usage and this is typically under adult supervision.

Work and education

Many of the accepted views of the generations matched the results of my survey, with some nuances and a few surprises. As expected, younger generations do want frequent feedback

– Gen Z leading with 'as often as possible' – but a portion of Millennials turned out to be satisfied with monthly or bi-weekly feedback, which isn't as high as the stereotype predicted.

The big surprise came in the question about ambition. Although Millennials and Gen Z topped the ambition scale, the number of Boomers and Gen Xers who described themselves as still ambitious was higher than expected.

Other anomalies

When it came to adopting new technology, the Silent Generation did indeed cluster heavily in 'In the middle' or 'One of the last", with only a small fraction reporting being 'The first' (see the 'Respondents' willingness to try new things' chart on page 122). It was surprising to see that Gen Alpha was slightly less likely to say 'The first' than the stereotype indicated; many placed themselves 'In the middle' instead. This suggests that while younger people are often adventurous, they may not see themselves as the absolute first to jump in. The youngest groups (Gen Z and Gen Alpha) were still more adventurous than older groups, but the actual difference between Gen X, Millennials and Gen Z was narrower than the stereotype would imply.

The big surprise was the extent to which each generation picks up on non-verbal communication (see page 117). Gen Alpha's survey results suggest they have better non-verbal skills than predicted, with more individuals than expected saying 'Very well'. Although the Silent Generation were near the lower end, 25 per cent still said 'Very well'. Millennials showed the highest proportion of 'Very well' at 38 per cent, which is close to what was expected, judging by the stereotypical view.

Interpreting the comparison

A high percentage of over-60s (Boomers and Silent Generation) do indeed stick to more traditional and expected communication patterns. However, a notable number are active on digital platforms, especially when nudged by family.

Meanwhile, in younger cohorts (Gen Z, Gen Alpha), the stereotype that they're hyper-digital is only partially validated, with the survey data showing a meaningful fraction appreciate offline communication. Some reported that they recognise the constraints that hamper constant digital usage. This reality leads to between 40 and 50 per cent aligning with typical stereotypes, so fewer than half always match the 'digital everything' narrative.

Reasons for people not matching their generational stereotypes

As discussed in Chapter 3, we're influenced by far more than our birth year. I talked about the Five Circles of Generational Influence, whereby within every generation there are factors like geography, immediate environment or simply personal preference that will greatly influence communication behaviour.

Family, school and workplace influences have a great impact on all of us. Younger cohorts might adopt calling or emailing if that's how parents or teachers want to communicate, and older cohorts might use social media if grandchildren or colleagues push them to do so.

As I also explained in Chapter 3, a big factor for all generations is the life stages that they go through. Looking at the generations in 2025, the youngest Gen Zers are still at secondary school and have yet to catch up with the older members of their cohort, who have been through school, higher education and a number of years already under their belt in the workplace. Meanwhile, young Gen Xers are just 45 while the oldest are turning 60 and therefore seeing retirement not far ahead – in fact some have already retired or gone part time. A generation's focus will change as it gets older, which will have a major impact on the attitudes of this generation and the way they communicate.

One of the biggest influences will be technological shifts, such as during the pandemic, which accelerated certain remote or hybrid approaches such as Zoom calls, that older generations embraced more than many would have predicted.

Finally, things, times and people change. Post-Covid, there has been an increased concern over privacy, data overload and mental health. This has led to many Gen Z and Millennials opting for 'digital detox' times, defying the idea they are always online.

Caveats and limitations

Many people straddle generations, creating 'cuspers'. For example, people like me born in 1963, 1964 or 1965 straddle the Gen X and Baby Boomer generations and therefore will not be as 'typical' as someone born in the middle of the generational cohort. Clearly a person's communication preferences don't change because they are the very first of a generation. This means by taking the literal cut-off years we have blurred the lines of preferences.

How stereotypical are we?

So finally, here's the answer you were looking for. This is a condensed summary of how frequently each cohort's actual responses matched the stereotypes typically assigned to them.

Silent	72 per cent
Baby Boomer	65 per cent
Gen X	58 per cent
Millennials (Gen Y)	63 per cent
Gen Z	70 per cent
Gen Alpha	68 per cent

In many cases, the data from my survey showed noticeable divergence from stereotypes. Some older respondents more fully embrace technology than some may have expected, while many younger respondents appreciate phone calls or in-person contact more than popular narratives suggest. Meanwhile, a portion of each group does follow the 'classic' pattern, producing these approximate percentages.

Older generations do exhibit many classic traits by favouring phone calls and are more cautious around social media. While they are slower to adopt new technology, more are digitally involved than the stereotype implies.

Roughly half of Gen X fit the classic portrayal as a 'bridge', and a similar proportion of Millennials are indeed 'digital integrators'. Meanwhile, the other half of each of these two generations diverges.

Finally, Gen Z and Gen Alpha illustrate that while many born after 1997 fulfil the 'digital native' label, a substantial portion values face-to-face contact, phone or voice calls, or are restricted by adult rules. They don't unilaterally 'live online' as the stereotype might suggest.

Overall, these findings from the analysis through AI suggest that when it comes to communication, generational stereotypes hold partial truth, with between 58 and 70 per cent of each generational group in my survey aligning with typical expectations. As a guesstimate, if you weight the results to take into account the number of respondents in each generation (outlined in Chapter 11) who took part in my survey, you can say that out of the data sample of 4,067, the proportion who are (on average) stereotypical of their generation is 65 per cent. This also means that each generation's capacity to contradict generalisations is 35 per cent.

When it comes to deciding if we are stereotypical or not, it's important to remember that the questions in the survey were focused purely on communication, and that this was a particular sample of people who, although they were spread across socioeconomic groups, are not necessarily fully representative. This means that although 65 per cent of those questioned in the survey may communicate in the way we might have expected, that doesn't mean we are all stereotypical to that degree. There are so many other aspects to our daily lives and attitudes that the survey didn't look at. This all adds to the complexity of understanding generations, so yes, we truly are framed by our generation and not defined by it.

Section 4

What next?

20 Thriving in a multi-generational workforce

Taking a snapshot of the generations in 2024 has been fascinating. So what can you do with what the two surveys have revealed? Our society is changing and evolving, as are our places of work, play and the home. Like time, no generation will stand still, so it's important to be mindful as we look at Generation Z moving into the workplace that in 50 years' time, they will be the same generation but preparing for retirement. In the meantime, they will go through the various life stages.

In Chapter 2, I talked about the huge benefits of understanding communication differences between generations and Section 3 explored exactly how the different generations communicate today. So, what can we all do to flourish in a multigenerational workforce and bridge the generational communication gap?

One of the big issues in the workplace today is the debate about hybrid working, with many companies mandating a return to the office for part or, in some cases, all of the week. I agree that there are huge benefits to everyone spending time in the office to enhance learning and develop professional work relationships. A lot of pressure has been put on younger employees to come into the office but the survey revealed that older Gen Zers actually feel more productive in the office, so they want to come in. After all, this is where watercooler conversations take place as well as learning by osmosis. The challenge is that if Gen Z's superiors (usually Millennials or Gen X) aren't in the office, they can question the value of coming in. Organisations can make a big difference by creating FOMO (fear of missing out) to combat HOGO (hassle of going out). In other words, by creating an environment where staff of all generations want to come into the office. Russ Lidstone, president of Inizio Engage XD, told me how their organisation works hard at creating the right atmosphere in their offices. He told me of numerous initiatives, including innovative working spaces, breakout rooms, kitchen and social spaces, after-work activities and socials. This has been so successful that 90 per cent of employees are in the office at least four days a week – by choice.

To help organisations develop a positive plan to bridge the generation gap in the workplace, I have brought together the results of my surveys with my other research and experience from working in different workplace environments to suggest ten key strategies that I believe will create a greater level of generational cohesion in the workplace.

The first action should come from an organisation's leadership and that is to recognise there is a real need for policies that bridge this gap. For most organisations these will be the foundation of an intergenerational policy document. Most businesses will have risk management, environment, sustainability, data privacy, diversity and inclusion and other policies to ensure compliance with relevant regulations in their industry as well as promote best practice. Surely a policy that considers generational diversity should also be considered by any progressive company. These ten strategies could feature in any intergenerational policy.

1. Establish the foundations of shared values and mutual respect

Before introducing specific actions, it's vital to set the stage by understanding why generational cohesion matters. According to my Generations in the Workplace Study 2023, 66 per cent of HR professionals acknowledged that communication across generations is a significant challenge in their businesses. Many respondents highlighted employees who often 'cluster' around colleagues from their own age group – a phenomenon sometimes called generational clustering. According to the 'Empowerment among Generations' study in 2017 by Usha Singh and Daniel Weimar, this clustering can reinforce misunderstandings about each other's communication preferences and skills, leading to reduced cooperation and, ultimately, diminished productivity. The central realisation is that employees of all generations value clarity, respect and efficiency in communication. Everyone wants to work where they feel their voice is heard and their abilities are recognised. The differences lie in how each generation prefers to achieve that clarity, whether it is through face-to-face conversations, concise emails, instant messages or a combination of channels.

One way to achieve this is an organisation-wide awareness campaign. This could take the form of a brief, accessible presentation on generational diversity and the benefits of having multiple age groups in the workplace. The campaign should include short videos or personal stories from employees across different generations, highlighting positive collaboration experiences. This content could be circulated via internal newsletters, intranet platforms or team briefings – in other words through all the different channels a company's employees will engage with.

Another effective strategy is to run generational awareness workshops, which can promote cross-generational understanding. As Rachele Focardi points out in her book *Reframing Generational Stereotypes* (2021), 'Workshops can provide a "brave space" where employees are able to have robust discussions.' Simply put, according to *Simply HR* (2025), these sessions can 'lead to improved communication, a reduction in conflicts, and increased productivity'.

Many organisations will have something along the lines of a 'charter of respect' and this could include a short, bullet-point list emphasising mutual respect, openness to learning and the value each generation brings. This charter could be posted in communal areas or on digital platforms so it remains a visible reminder of the organisation's ethos.

Inclusive language is essential to ensure mutual respect in the workplace and every communication must contain language that will be understood by everyone. It's all too easy to use language familiar to your own generation and forget that other generations may feel excluded if they don't understand certain terminology or vocabulary. Many organisations will already have policies surrounding industry jargon and language that is inclusive for a diverse workforce, so it's simply a matter of including generational language in the policy.

The tone for any initiative is set by the leadership team, so it's important that management openly discusses the importance of intergenerational cooperation and examples of successful generational collaboration during town halls, Q&A sessions or in internal videos. This will help signal that these values are integral, not just 'feel-good' add-ons.

2. Tangle your teams and break down generational silos

As the two surveys I commissioned have reinforced, people often prefer to associate with their own generation both socially and in the workplace. This generational clustering is a real tendency, and it is driven by shared experiences, communication styles and values, which foster a sense of common identity, comfort and understanding. Individuals within the same generation share significant historical and cultural experiences, such as technological advancements, economic conditions and major global events (as discussed in Section 2 of this book). They also have common cultural touchpoints, such as music and television shows, which enhance communication and bonding.

In the workplace, a study published in the *Journal of Organizational Behavior* (Mao et al 2021) found that employees often form generational cohorts within organisations, seeking colleagues from their age group for support and collaboration. This can be a challenge for an organisation, as seen in the Deloitte 2024 Gen Z and Millennial Survey, where it was found that generational differences can lead to workplace tension, prompting individuals to gravitate toward peers with similar values and work styles.

I have developed the concept of 'tangling teams', where an organisation is encouraged to orchestrate cross-generational collaboration so that employees learn from one another. Splitting up those naturally formed clusters may seem counterproductive and certainly people need to step out of their comfort zones to do it, but the benefits for growth are huge.

To achieve this, when committees or project teams are brought together, look at ways you can bring in a mix of Baby Boomers, Gen X, Gen Y (Millennials) and Gen Z employees. An organisation could facilitate a rotating leadership structure in these teams so that each member, regardless of seniority or age, occasionally leads discussions or subprojects. This can work hand in hand with a buddy system where employees from different generations pair up for certain tasks. For example, a Gen Z digital native could guide a Baby Boomer on new software, while a Baby Boomer might share in-depth knowledge about long-standing client relationships, negotiation skills or proven industry best practices. This blends well with the concept of mutual mentoring (see point number 5).

Other opportunities to tangle teams could be with hosted lunchtime learning sessions. This is where one person from each generation demonstrates a skill such as business writing, using a new social media platform or problem-solving strategies they have developed over the years. This will foster a culture of mutual respect, showing that every group has unique expertise to contribute.

3. Confront unconscious bias by re-evaluating assumptions about age

Many organisations fall into the trap of labelling employees by generation, assuming that 'older equals less tech savvy' or 'younger equals immature with no corporate loyalty'. My surveys have made it clear that these stereotypes don't always stand up to scrutiny, particularly when some Baby Boomer respondents declared they were just as enthusiastic about video calls as their younger colleagues. Unconscious bias across age groups reduces inclusion and stifles innovation. When employees feel pigeonholed, they're less likely to innovate or speak up. However, as neuroscientist Dr Lynda Shaw told me on my podcast, 'We can't get rid of unconscious bias, but we can manage it.'

This is where unconscious bias training comes in – but it does need to include generational bias. Optional or mandatory training on unconscious bias should be part of every organisation's training programme and it should include dealing with age-based stereotypes. An effective way to challenge these assumptions is to include real-world case studies such as an older employee who successfully adopts new technology or a younger employee's adept face-to-face negotiation.

Part of the unconscious bias training should be to encourage employees to speak up when they encounter or sense age-based biases, whether that's in performance reviews, daily communication or team dynamics. There could also be short, anonymous surveys or digital suggestion boxes where people can highlight generational friction points without fear of repercussion.

It's always great when an organisation can regularly highlight examples of cross-generational success in internal communications. By celebrating real examples, individuals are reminded that assumptions about others' abilities based solely on age are often misplaced.

4. Personalise communication training

The communication survey showed that while many younger staff favour quick, informal messaging, many older colleagues may prefer face-to-face discussions or more formal emails. The challenge here is to avoid making the assumption that these patterns apply to everyone. That would be a mistake because the survey also highlighted that even within the same generation, preferences vary according to personal style and the situation. A Baby Boomer might text frequently, while a Millennial could choose meticulous emails for complex issues. The reality is that one size does not fit all and for training to be effective, options to personalise it should be considered.

It's natural for people to favour the tool that suits the task at hand – if it's available. This is why training needs to be flexible in allowing individuals to choose modules and delivery methods that are relevant to their needs.

A way to do this is to offer short, focused workshops. Taking communication as an example, modules tailored to specific methods and purposes of communication could be developed. For example:

- *Module* A: Creating concise, attention-grabbing emails.

- *Module* B: Getting the best out of instant messaging platforms (Slack, Microsoft Teams).

- *Module* C: Effective virtual meeting etiquette (Zoom, Teams, Google Meet).

- *Module* D: Conducting constructive feedback sessions (in person or via video).

This would allow employees to sign up for the modules that were most relevant to their work style or the tools they feel least confident using.

The training team could adopt a simple 'communication matrix' that helps staff choose the right tool for each situation. Using the communication training example again, a quick question that needs an immediate answer might work best via instant messenger, whereas a complex topic requiring detailed discussion might require a face-to-face meeting or a phone call.

For new tools or platforms, managers could sponsor hands-on tutorials where more experienced users are paired with novices so that skill gaps close quickly. This approach also encourages employees to swap knowledge organically, reinforcing cross-generational relationships.

5. Foster cross-generational mutual mentorship

A great concept is reverse mentoring, where the traditional mentoring roles are reversed so it's not just the senior person mentoring the junior one, but also the other way round. However, a phrase that is considered more appropriate today is mutual mentoring. A standout recommendation from multiple respondents in the survey was the use of mentorship programmes to bridge age gaps. For instance, a tech-savvy

Generation Z employee can mentor a Generation X manager on leveraging social media platforms for brand promotion, while the manager shares insights on strategic planning and industry-specific knowledge.

Mentorship benefits both parties. The 'seasoned' mentor feels valued for sharing expertise, and the less experienced mentee gains knowledge that might otherwise be inaccessible. In effect, the mentor becomes the mentee and vice versa, so in mutual mentorship, the more traditional roles can often be switched, which helps to challenge stereotypes about older staff being 'stuck in their ways'. Mentorship can also manifest itself in many ways, as Steve Butler says in his book *Manage the Gap* (2019): 'Mentoring doesn't have to be about direction; it can be about cooperation and it can be fostered informally through social networks.'

To set up a mutual mentoring scheme, employees are invited to participate as either mentors or mentees, or both, making it clear that everyone has something to learn and something to teach. Those mentoring are offered basic training on effective coaching and mentees are shown how to maximise these opportunities. This works best when staff in more senior roles (executive managers, department heads), who are possibly older, are encouraged to pair up with junior, possibly younger, employees who excel in digital platforms, social media strategy or emerging industry trends.

Monthly or fortnightly check-ins for these pairs to exchange insights are essential and each pair should set a clear objective. This could be 'By the end of this quarter, we will have built a new skill set for X' or 'We will develop a refined approach to client updates'. Setting specific goals ensures that mentorship programmes don't become just a well-intentioned but unfocused chat.

6. Cultivate a culture of learning

Cohesion among generations often depends on an organisation's broader culture. A culture that values ongoing development and curiosity will naturally encourage employees to look beyond their generational clusters and learn from each other. A culture that does not place a premium on learning might, by mistake, increase generational divisions as employees see no reason to adopt new ways or share their own expertise.

Curiosity and respect for knowledge are crucial to bridging generational divides. The survey showed that older and younger workers alike can be highly receptive to new methods if they see a direct benefit or a clear link to their roles.

The way to achieve this is to allocate a specific amount of time to skills training that each person feels comfortable with. This could be attending a seminar, taking an online course or engaging in conferences. Some organisations call this a 'personal development budget'. Managers should encourage employees to pick something that genuinely resonates with their career aims, not just the organisation's immediate needs.

Cross-departmental exchanges provide opportunities for short-term 'swaps'. There are also shadowing programmes, where employees from different departments (and often different age profiles) spend a few days or weeks learning about each other's roles. This breaks monotony, broadens skill sets and fosters greater empathy for colleagues' challenges and workload.

Finally, management and HR departments can encourage employees to set up clubs or interest groups such as reading circles, tech clubs and language exchanges. These groups can bring people from different generations together around a common interest and can be facilitated by the organisation by providing a meeting space and a budget for refreshments.

7. Tailor feedback and performance reviews

A big topic in both of my surveys was feedback and reviews. As I discovered, different generations can have contrasting expectations for how feedback should be given. For example, some Baby Boomers and Gen Xers may appreciate a face-to-face meeting every few months, whereas many Gen Y (Millennials) and Gen Z employees prefer more frequent, informal check-ins to stay aligned with rapidly evolving objectives. Yet again, though, this doesn't go along strict generation lines, so a one-size-fits-all approach won't work. Increasing feedback frequency may suit some staff but alienate others. A flexible but structured approach to feedback ensures that people feel supported rather than micromanaged.

The key here is to allow employees the ability to self-select feedback frequency (within reason) as this can dramatically improve engagement and reduce staff turnover, particularly among younger workers who generally value more frequent input.

The way to achieve this is for managers to ask employees during onboarding or annual reviews how frequently they would like check-ins (weekly, bi-weekly, monthly) and in what format (in person, email summary, phone call). An organisation still needs a standard such as mandatory quarterly performance reviews, but this extra level of flexibility will be appreciated by all employees. This does mean that managers and team leaders need to be trained in how to listen actively and ask open-ended questions so that feedback sessions feel collaborative rather than top down. Employees should also be encouraged to come prepared with questions for their manager. This two-way flow fosters a sense of partnership.

Regardless of how the feedback or review is delivered, there should be a quick written recap of each session, highlighting agreed-upon goals, any concerns raised and next steps. This helps people track progress and avoids miscommunication.

8. Encourage transparency from management

Survey comments revealed that employees across all generations want leadership to be visible and know how their work contributes to the organisation's broader goals. This was particularly the case for Gen Y (Millennials) and Gen Z. Meanwhile, older generations often seek reassurance that their decades of expertise remain valued. Transparency, then, is a universal need.

Transparency means regular updates on company performance, strategic objectives and policy changes. This reduces uncertainty and helps staff see where they fit in – I often say KPI also stands for 'keep people informed'. Transparency fosters trust, irrespective of age bracket.

These updates can take the form of regular town halls and Q&A sessions, which could be quarterly or monthly. They should always allow for plenty of interaction and opportunities to ask questions. Again, this is particularly important for Gen Z, so these events should allow for both in-person and livestream options, with a recording, transcript and closed captions available for remote, neurodivergent and other differently abled staff. These updates should be easy to attend and feel less tell and more share. Employees should be encouraged to submit questions anonymously beforehand – this may help those who are uncomfortable speaking out in front of others.

Important updates should be available in multiple formats, including email, instant messaging, the company intranet or a shared noticeboard. With the multiple ways people like to communicate, it's important to cover all bases so that employees can access information in the way they prefer. Updates could include short video updates from senior leadership as many employees appreciate seeing and hearing directly from top-level staff.

Organisations can encourage two-way transparency by inviting employees to share their thoughts on upcoming initiatives, either through structured brainstorming sessions, online idea boards or smaller focus groups. It's important to demonstrate that suggestions from any generation are welcome and can directly influence company decisions. These suggestions can be followed up with success stories and acknowledgement of where ideas and initiatives have come from.

9. Embrace multiple communication channels and adapt to context

Using multiple communication channels, or omnichannel communication, has been mentioned in some of the other strategies but it's such an important element for every organisation to consider. One recurring insight from my survey is that while certain generations lean toward particular communication channels, everyone ultimately appreciates well-chosen, thoughtful communication. For instance, a text message may be wonderful for a quick heads-up but might be misread when conveying emotional or nuanced feedback. It's also important to bear in mind that an individual's favoured method of communication may not, as the survey data has shown, fit with the stereotype.

It's not just the communication channel; it's also a case of matching the channel to the message. A sensitive discussion might call for a face-to-face approach, while an urgent question may benefit from an instant chat. An overview of project milestones can be well suited to email, while a significant announcement deserves a group meeting.

So, how do you determine the right approach to contextualising communication? The first stage is to define communication channel guidelines by creating a clear reference document, which ideally will be co-created with a mix of employees and managers of different levels and generations explaining when each channel might be most appropriate. Emails, phone calls, instant messaging, video chats or face-to-face meetings will have their strengths in certain situations. The suitability and context will also depend on the audience. The reference document should be short and practical. For example: 'Use instant messaging for quick clarifications; if the issue is complicated or personal, opt for a conversation or phone call.'

When it comes to training, too many assumptions are made regarding communication, so being specific about best and preferred practice avoids any misunderstanding. Whether it's setting up a group chat, scheduling video conferences or structuring an email, confidence in the tool fosters better communication.

Clearly the leadership and management should exemplify these guidelines. If a manager consistently sends lengthy feedback via text, it undermines the recommended best practices. In team meetings it's helpful to highlight examples of when a certain channel was used to great effect.

10. Measure, refine and celebrate progress

Finally, a plan is only as good as its execution and ongoing refinement. Measuring progress and then celebrating milestones will keep everyone motivated. It also reassures all generations that this initiative isn't a passing trend but a structured approach to building a better workplace. Continuous improvement keeps generational cohesion from becoming a tick-box exercise and regular measurement allows the organisation to spot areas of improvement and refine the plan.

The first way to measure progress is to conduct short, regular surveys (monthly or quarterly) to capture how employees feel about communication quality and team cohesion. It's a good idea to make these surveys anonymous to encourage honesty. Focus on questions such as 'Do you feel your communication preferences are respected?' or 'Have you seen improvements in cross-generational teamwork?'

Where possible, establish tangible indicators. For example, track how often cross-generational teams are formed, measure staff turnover rates (especially of younger staff who can be quick to leave if unsatisfied) and review the frequency of mentorship pairings. Then align these KPIs with broader organisational goals, such as linking better communication to higher client satisfaction or improved project completion times.

Finally, when you identify improvements such as a reduction in communication-related conflicts or higher satisfaction from new hires, share these results widely. It's so effective to recognise teams or individuals who have excelled in bridging generational gaps, whether it's a Baby Boomer stepping out of their comfort zone and successfully adopting new technology or a Gen Z employee showcasing new ways to incorporate formal business etiquette.

Bringing it all together to thrive in a multigenerational workforce

One powerful takeaway from the Communication Habits and Preferences 2024 survey is that while generational differences in communication styles do exist, these distinctions needn't become insurmountable barriers. Organisations thrive when they treat staff as individuals, acknowledging varied preferences while providing tools and structures that encourage collaboration. By tangling teams, addressing unconscious bias, offering flexible communication training and fostering a culture of learning, you create an environment where employees feel genuinely valued for who they are and for what they can learn from their colleagues.

Remember, each generation has something vital to bring to the table. Baby Boomers have historical knowledge of the business and deep relationship-building experience. Generation X often functions as a bridge, adept with both traditional methods and new technologies. Millennials, or Generation Y, introduce agility, digital fluency and a fresh perspective on company values. Generation Z, the youngest cohort in the workforce, has grown up in the digital era and often nudges everyone to adopt faster, more efficient online tools. When these talents and strengths converge, the synergy can be profound. Moreover, the assumption that older employees are always slow to adopt new technology or that younger staff can't handle face-to-face interactions is continually upended by real-world examples. The most successful teams create a culture that fosters the best traits of each group rather than forcing assimilation to a single norm.

From an individual's perspective, regardless of age, adopting an open mindset is such an important aspect of bridging the generation gap. Having the ability to adjust habits and learn new skills from colleagues (even those much younger or older) accelerates personal development. It also boosts interpersonal respect. If everyone in an organisation were to embrace 'I can learn from you, and you can learn from me', the possibilities for growth would multiply. Underpinning any strong communication plan are empathy and a willingness to adapt. Empathy suggests pausing to ask 'Why does my Baby Boomer colleague prefer a face-to-face chat over an instant message?' or 'Why might my Gen Z teammate be frustrated by lengthy email threads?'

By understanding personal comfort zones and the reasoning behind them, teams can work on compromises that reduce friction. For instance, by sending a short heads-up message before organising a longer phone chat, you meet the needs of both the instant communication advocate and the colleague who values the depth of a spoken conversation.

A constant theme in this book has been that workplace communication is seldom one size fits all. Whether to schedule an in-person meeting, make a phone call or send an instant message depends on context. Over time, these day-to-day decisions shape workplace culture, reinforcing an organisation's broader stance on respect, clarity and efficiency.

Ultimately, the reward for implementing an intergenerational communication policy is a workplace that harnesses the collective strengths of all its members. That environment is more likely to retain talented individuals (irrespective of age), attract top candidates who value progressive and inclusive cultures, and deliver better results to clients and stakeholders. Moreover, employees – from the newest recruit to the most veteran manager – are more likely to find greater satisfaction in their roles when they work in an atmosphere where each person's perspective is respected and each voice can be heard.

Achieving cohesion among the four generations in the workplace – Baby Boomers, Generation X, Millennials (Gen Y) and Generation Z – is no small endeavour. Differences in communication styles, life experiences and even the historical events that shaped these age groups can easily lead to friction or misunderstanding. However, as my Communication Habits and Preferences 2024 survey demonstrates, these differences can also be a valuable source of innovation and learning when approached with respect and openness.

By establishing shared values, breaking down generational clustering, actively confronting unconscious biases, personalising communication training and nurturing cross-generational mentorship, organisations can significantly improve day-to-day interactions. When combined with a transparent leadership style, context-appropriate communication channels and ongoing measurement of progress, these strategies form the core of a dynamic, future-focused culture.

It is a journey, not a quick fix. Change will require support from management and buy-in at every level, from HR specialists and team leaders to new hires and experienced veterans. Yet the benefits of a cohesive, multigenerational workforce, where members share knowledge, respect each other's preferences and rally around shared values, will be felt not only in productivity and innovation but also in a workplace culture where everyone, across the generational spectrum, genuinely thrives.

By taking these actions, organisations and individuals ensure they do more than just 'cope' with generational differences. They unlock the potential for synergy, creativity and personal growth. They have the opportunity to discover the benefits of a truly multigenerational workforce. A workforce that can be dynamic and ever evolving.

Yes, it might require effort and conscious intent, but the rewards are immeasurable.

21 Final words

In this book I have tried to show how much we can learn by studying the generations and the various elements that have shaped their beliefs and behaviours. From the outset, I wanted to encourage readers to move away from the stereotypical perceptions of each generation. As you will have discovered, there are generational patterns, and these can be helpful to identify because by understanding them we can connect better with other generations at home, at work and socially. However, it's also important to remember that patterns can only go so far when trying to understand someone's communication preferences, so it is incredibly important to treat people on an individual basis. If you make assumptions about people because of generational stereotypes you might miss out on a new friendship or a great new team member for your organisation.

In Section 2, I looked at the generally accepted views on the six different generations and was keen to give you an understanding of their backgrounds to help you understand why each generation has the characteristics it does. It's so much easier to have empathy for one another if you understand the background and development of each generation as they grew up.

Then, in Section 3, I shared the analysis of the two surveys, the first looking at the perspective of HR professionals on communication in the workplace and the second at the detail of communication preferences across generations and socioeconomic groups. The first study indicated that most organisations would benefit from improved intergenerational understanding and communication (which is why, in Chapter 20, I outlined some principles that organisations could adopt to facilitate this). The first survey also showed there are clear differences in communication preferences between generations as well as attitudes towards feedback, comfort with hierarchy and loyalty patterns.

Many of those findings were consistent with the findings of my second survey, Communication Habits and Preferences Survey 2024, which revealed clear generational differences in communication but also highlighted some surprising anomalies such as, while Gen Z and Millennials dominate text-based communication, 22 per cent of Gen Z actually prefer voice notes over texts, appreciating the speed and expressiveness. As expected, Gen X and Baby Boomers remain email and phone call loyalists, but 34 per cent of Baby Boomers did report using WhatsApp groups frequently, mainly for family connections, which challenges the stereotype that Boomers struggle with digital communication. As one Boomer participant shared: 'WhatsApp is great for keeping in touch with my kids and grandkids.'

Social media also followed predictable generational trends, with 85 per cent of Gen Z and Millennials using it daily. However, 16 per cent of Silent Generation respondents (78+) reported regular Facebook use, mainly for staying in touch with family. A Silent Generation respondent commented: 'I use Facebook to see what my grandchildren are up to – it's wonderful.'

In workplace communication, Gen Z and Millennials prefer instant messaging platforms like Slack, yet 17 per cent of Gen Z reported preferring email for formal communication, valuing it as a record-keeping tool. One young professional said: 'For work, I still like email – it keeps things official.'

These findings reinforce that while communication preferences are largely generational, personal habits and technological adaptability create surprising exceptions, making intergenerational communication more nuanced than expected.

Looking to the future

Future generations will be shaped by a multitude of factors. One of those is the increasing societal pressures on all of us, but more than ever before on Generation Alpha and soon-to-be Generation Beta. With the advancement of technology and the devices we use to access apps and social media, younger generations are being exposed to these influences at an earlier age. This makes it harder for parents to oversee – so, as seven-year-old Molly Wright says in her TED talk: 'Healthy development depends on connecting, talking, playing, a healthy home, and community. All of this helps our brains and us reach our full potential.' This certainly supports what Jonathan Haidt alluded to in *The Anxious Generation* (2024), where he advocated 'real world playing' as opposed to 'phone-based playing' and learning that is synchronous as opposed to asynchronous, so that younger generations can benefit from a shared in-person experience.

Managing future workforces

Like parenting, I believe management has never been so complex and often challenging, requiring a greater level of people skills than ever before. In the workplace, managers need to have a stronger understanding of their teams and look at the amount of feedback they are giving. They need to understand the modern workplace and all the nuances that didn't exist in the pre-digital age. Gone are the days of one-size-fits-all management techniques. What is needed today is bespoke management. My suggestions in Chapter 20 should help to break down generational silos and bring people from different generations together. Yes, a bespoke approach is harder, but it is the only effective way to increase employee satisfaction – which will in turn lead to greater productivity, reduced attrition and an increase in the bottom line. For everyone in the workplace today, having a greater appreciation and understanding of each other's generation should be a goal. This can be helped with additional training and by having an intergenerational policy.

Every workplace is unique, but the patterns and insights from my surveys can serve as a valuable roadmap for anyone looking to navigate the intersection of generations. When

HR professionals tune in to these nuances – offering flexible approaches to communication and recognising the common ground that all employees share – they stand a much better chance of building teams that not only coexist but genuinely thrive together.

Whether you're an HR manager, a seasoned leader, or someone just stepping into your first professional role, the best advice is to keep your eyes and ears open. Ask how your colleagues want to communicate. Be ready to adjust your style. And most importantly, stay curious, because every generation brings something fresh to the table – and the payoff from understanding those contributions can be enormous for your organisation's long-term success.

That's the power of truly understanding and embracing generational diversity. By meeting each other halfway in how we talk, collaborate and learn, we reduce friction at home, in places of study and the workplace. We can also pave the way for new ideas, healthier relationships and a more inclusive environment for everyone where we see social and professional relationships between generations as personal rather than a process.

My Five Principles for Stronger Intergenerational Relationships

I'm going to finish by sharing a model I use to help everyone have better intergenerational relationships. It's called the Five Principles for Stronger Intergenerational Relationships, and it applies to the workplace, at home and in social settings. It also applies to all of us regardless of our generation and in both directions. In other words, it is as much from Gen Y (Millennials) to Gen Alpha and it is from Gen Z to Gen X, and so on.

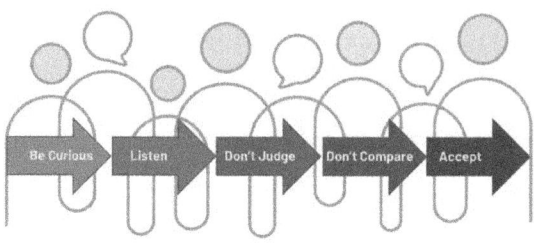

Be curious

Curiosity fosters understanding and dismantles assumptions. Instead of relying on stereotypes, approach intergenerational interactions with genuine interest. As psychotherapist Shelley Bridgeman told me on my *Generationally Speaking* podcast: 'Start with curiosity – ask what matters to them – don't assume you know.'

Ask open-ended questions to learn about others' experiences, perspectives and motivations. Curiosity encourages learning from different generational viewpoints, making relationships richer and more dynamic. This will help uncover shared values and common ground while encouraging a mindset of continual learning from different generations. It will build stronger and more meaningful connections by valuing individual stories and experiences.

Listen

Active listening is crucial in bridging generational divides. It's not just about hearing words but about truly understanding the message behind them. In other words, really listen. As the actor and communication advocate Alan Alda said in his book *If I Understood You, Would I Have This Look on My Face?* (2017): 'Real conversation can't happen if listening is just my waiting for you to finish talking', which highlights the importance of active listening. By giving your full attention, avoiding interrupting and reflecting on what's being said before responding, you can reduce miscommunication and misunderstandings. Active listening also demonstrates respect and appreciation for different perspectives while creating a space for all voices to be heard and valued.

Don't judge

Each generation has been shaped by unique historical, social and cultural influences. Although it can be very tempting, avoid making snap judgements about someone's values, work ethic or preferences based on their age or background. Instead, seek to understand why people think and act the way they do. As Claudette Dawson said on my podcast *Generationally Speaking*, 'If you find yourself tempted to make a judgement, just ask another question instead.' Being judgemental is one of the biggest causes of generational conflict. By avoiding it you'll promote a feeling of inclusivity and respect. It will also encourage open-mindedness and flexibility in relationships.

Don't compare

It's natural to see the world through your own experiences and use phrases like 'When I was your age...' or 'When I started work...' or the dreaded 'In my day...' The problem is that by constantly comparing one generation to another, you'll create division. Whatever discussion you're having, the reality is there probably is no comparison, because people and circumstances have changed so much. Instead of saying 'Your generation doesn't get...', focus on appreciating differences rather than seeing them as a negative. This way you'll encourage a positive exchange of ideas instead of making it a competition that will help each generation to appreciate their unique contributions. You'll also reduce resentment while promoting understanding.

Accept we are all different

Sometimes things just are the way they are, and real intergenerational harmony comes from embracing diversity. No single approach, preference or value system is inherently better than another – they are just different. Recognising and respecting these differences allows for mutual growth and stronger relationships. Accepting that we are all different will cultivate empathy and deeper understanding. It will also encourage adaptability in personal and professional settings.

By applying these five principles, individuals and organisations can create more inclusive, understanding and effective intergenerational relationships. The key is to approach differences with an open mind, value each person's unique perspective and focus on connection rather than division.

There are no shortcuts to bridging generational differences, but my wish is that as a result of reading this book you will see generational patterns rather than relying on generational stereotypes. After all, as I have said throughout, we are framed by our generation, not defined by it – and remembering that will hopefully reduce generational stereotyping. Sure, it takes a bit more work to really understand each other's generational and personal perspective, but the benefits will be worth it.

References

Throughout the book I refer to episodes of my podcast, *Alastair Greener Generationally Speaking* – these can all be found at generationallyspeaking.co.uk/podcasts

The two Present Yourself surveys, Generations in the Workplace Study 2023 and Communication Habits and Preferences 2024, can both be found at generationallyspeaking.co.uk/research

Introduction

Clifton, J & Ray, J (2025) 'Is a kinder world a happier one?'. Gallup, 19 March. URL: news.gallup.com/opinion/gallup/657998/kinder-world-happier-one.aspx

Codrington, G (2012) *Mind the Gap: Own your past, know your generation, choose your future*. Penguin.

Dynata Market Research. URL: dynata.com

Gallup (2025) 'World Happiness Report 2025'. URL: gallup.com/analytics/349487/world-happiness-report.aspx

Chapter 1

Lippert, J & Fetterolf, J (2025) 'Best age to get married, have a child, buy a home and retire? Here's what Americans say'. *Pew Research Center*, 19 March. URL: pewresearch.org/short-reads/2025/03/19/best-age-to-get-married-have-a-child-buy-a-home-and-retire-heres-what-americans-say

Mannheim, K (1923) 'The Problem of Generations'. In Kecskemeti, P, ed (1952) *Essays on the Sociology of Knowledge: Collected Works, Volume V*. Routledge.

Orwell, G (1945) 'Review of *A Coat of Many Colours: Occasional Essays* by Herbert Read'. In Orwell, S and Angus, I, eds (1968) *The Collected Essays, Journalism and Letters of George Orwell, Volume 4: In Front of Your Nose, 1945–1950*. URL: ia802204.us.archive.org/32/items/in.ernet. dli.2015.86561/2015.86561.The-Collected-Essays-Journalism-And-Letters-Of-George-Orwell-Vol-Iv_text.pdf

Parker, K (2023) 'How Pew Research Center will report on generations moving forward'. Pew Research Center, 22 May. URL: pewresearch.org/short-reads/2023/05/22/how-pew-research-center-will-report-on-generations-moving-forward

Pew Research Center (2019) 'Defining our six generations'. *Pew Trusts*, 8 February. URL: pewtrusts.org/en/research-and-analysis/data-visualizations/2019/defining-our-six-generations

Statista (2025a) 'Number of people aged 100 and older (centenarians) worldwide from 2000 to 2100'. URL: statista.com/statistics/996597/number-centenarians-worldwide

Statista (2025b) 'Employment rate in the United Kingdom from 1st quarter 2000 to 4th quarter 2024, by age group'. URL: statista.com/statistics/280228/uk-employment-rate-by-age-group

Strauss, W & Howe, N (1991) *Generations: The history of America's future, 1584 to 2069*. Morrow.

Chapter 2

Grammarly (2024) '2024 State of Business Communication: AI's potential to turn overload into impact'. Grammarly. URL: go.grammarly.com/thankyou/content/2024-SOBC-Report

Hinsliff, G (2024) '"I never want you around your grandchild": The families torn apart when adult children decide to go "no contact"'. *The Guardian*, 9 November. URL: theguardian.com/lifeandstyle/2024/nov/09/

the-families-torn-apart-when-adult-children-decide-to-go-no-contact

Koop, A (2021) 'Chart: How Gen Z employment levels compare in OECD countries'. World Economic Forum, 26 March. URL: weforum.org/stories/2021/03/gen-z-unemployment-chart-global-comparisons

Chapter 3

Baker, L A & Daniels, D (1990) 'Nonshared environmental influences and personality differences in adult twins'. *Journal of Personality and Social Psychology* 58(1). URL: doi. org/10.1037/0022-3514.58.1.103

Department for Education (2021) 'Study of early education and development (SEED)'. Gov.uk, 29 October. URL: www.gov. uk/government/collections/study-of-early-education-and-development-seed

Department for Environment, Food and Rural Affairs (Defra) (2025) 'Key Findings, Statistical Digest of Rural England'. Gov.uk. URL: www.gov.uk/government/statistics/key-findings-statistical-digest-of-rural-england/key-findings-statistical-digest-of-rural-england

Dr Lynda Shaw. URL: drlyndashaw.com

Federal Reserve History (2013) 'The Great Recession and its aftermath'. URL: federalreservehistory.org/essays/great-recession-and-its-aftermath

Guillén, M F (2023) *The Perennials: Unleashing the power of our postgenerational society*. Heligo Books.

Kemp, S (2024) 'Digital 2024: The United Kingdom'. *DataReportal*, 21 February. URL: datareportal.com/reports/digital-2024-united-kingdom

Pell, G (2015) 'Meet the Perennials'. *The What*, 1 January 2025. URL: thewhathq.substack.com/p/meet-the-perennials

Twenge, J M (2023) *The Generations: The real differences between Gen Z, Millennials, Gen X, Boomers and Silents – and what they mean for the future*. Atria Books.

Chapter 4

Bayley, J (2024) 'Pub closures highest for a decade in 2023'. *Harpers Wine & Spirit*, 18 March. URL: harpers.co.uk/news/fullstory.php/aid/32543/Pub_closures_highest_for_a_decade_in_2023.html

Beck, U (1986) *Risk Society: Towards a new modernity*. Sage Publications.

Bolton, P (2025) 'Research briefing: Higher education student numbers'. House of Commons Library, 25 March. URL: commonslibrary.parliament.uk/research-briefings/cbp-7857

Brokaw, T (1998) *The Greatest Generation*. Random House.

Coupland, D (1991) *Generation X: Tales for an Accelerated Culture*. St Martin's Press.

Covey, S R (1989) *The Seven Habits of Highly Effective People*. Simon & Schuster.

Giddens, A (1991) *Modernity and Self-Identity: Self and Society in the Late Modern Age*. Stanford University Press.

Haidt, J (2024) *The Anxious Generation: How the great rewiring of childhood is causing an epidemic of mental illness*. Penguin Random House.

Johnson, J & Newport, E (1989) 'Critical period effects in language learning: The influence of maturational state on the acquisition of English as a second language'. *Cognitive Psychology* 21(1). URL: doi.org/10.1016/0010-0285(89)90003-0

Mannheim, K (1923) – see Chapter 1.

Thompson, D (2025) 'The anti-social century'. *The Atlantic*, 8 January. URL: theatlantic.com/magazine/archive/2025/02/american-loneliness-personality-politics/681091

United Nations (2024) 'World Population Prospects 2024: Summary of Results'. United Nations Department of Economic and Social Affairs Population Division. URL: population.un.org/wpp/assets/Files/WPP2024_Summary-of-Results.pdf

Wholesale Coffee Company (2023) 'UK set to have more coffee shops than pubs by 2030'. URL: wholesalecoffeecompany.

co.uk/blog/uk-set-to-have-more-coffee-shops-than-pubs-by-2030

Chapter 5

Booking.com (2025) 'Travel reinvented: Booking.com's 2025 travel predictions'. URL: booking.com/articles/travelpredictions2025.en-gb.html

CLIA (2025) '2023 global passenger report'. URL: cruising.org/resources/2023-global-passenger-report

Guinness World Records (2025) 'Oldest doctor (male)'. URL: guinnessworldrecords.com/world-records/75949-oldest-practicing-physician

HR News Editorial Team (2024) 'The benefits of age diversity in UK workplaces'. *HR News*. URL: hrnews.co.uk/the-benefits-of-age-diversity-in-uk-workplaces

Nobel Prize, The (2025) 'John B Goodenough: Facts'. URL: nobelprize.org/prizes/chemistry/2019/goodenough/facts

Pearson National Teaching Awards (2024) '2024 Gold Winners'. URL: teachingawards.com/2024-certificate-winners/2024-gold-winners

RBC (2019) 'SKI'ing – spending the kid's inheritance and other ways to manage what you leave behind'. Royal Bank, 24 January. URL: rbcroyalbank.com/en-ca/my-money-matters/goals-aspirations/retirement/will-and-estate-planning/skiing-spending-the-kids-inheritance-and-other-ways-to-manage-what-you-leave-behind

Statista (2025) 'Population share of generations in the United Kingdom from 1990 to 2023'. 8 January. URL: statista.com/statistics/528597/share-of-different-generations-in-the-united-kingdom-uk

Strauss & Howe (1991) – see Chapter 1.

Time (1951) 'People: The younger generation'. 5 November. URL: time.com/archive/6794406/people-the-younger-generation

UK Parliament (2025) 'The Education Act of 1944'.
URL: parliament.uk/about/living-heritage/
transformingsociety/livinglearning/school/overview/
educationact1944

US Department of Veterans Affairs (2024) 'About GI Bill
benefits'. VA.gov, 29 November. URL: va.gov/education/
about-gi-bill-benefits

Chapter 6

Active Financial Planners (2019) 'Baby boomers need financial
advice as many admit lack of investment knowledge and
confidence'. 8 April. URL: activefinancialplanners.co.uk/
our-thoughts/baby-boomers-need-financial-advice-
as-many-admit-lack-of-investment-knowledge-and-
confidence

Bolton, P (2012) 'Education: Historical statistics'. House of
Commons Library, 27 November. URL: researchbriefings.
files.parliament.uk/documents/SN04252/SN04252.pdf

Bureau of the Census (1958) 'Current population reports:
Population estimates'. 17 February. URL: www2.census.
gov/library/publications/1958/demographics/P25-173.pdf

CBI (2024) 'The European market for potential Baby Boomer
tourism'. URL: cbi.eu/market-information/tourism/baby-
boomer-tourism/market-potential

Fry, R & Braga, D (2023) 'Older workers are growing in
number and earning higher wages'. Pew Research
Center, 14 December. URL: pewresearch.org/
social-trends/2023/12/14/older-workers-are-growing-
in-number-and-earning-higher-wages

Jones, L & Tertilt, M (2006) 'An economic history of fertility in
the US: 1826–1960'. NBER Working Papers 12796, National
Bureau of Economic Research. URL: users.econ.umn.
edu/~lej/papers/empiricalfertilityDec06.pdf

Krueger, A O (2006) 'Evolution not revolution: The changing
role of the IMF in the global economy'. IMF, 23 February.
URL: imf.org/en/News/Articles/2015/09/28/04/53/
sp022306

Office for National Statistics (2015) 'Trends in births and deaths over the last century'. 15 July. URL: ons.gov.uk/peoplepopulationandcommunity/birthsdeathsandmarriages/livebirths/articles/trendsinbirthsanddeathsoverthelastcentury/2015-07-15

Office for National Statistics (2018) 'Living longer: how our population is changing and why it matters'. 13 August. URL: ons.gov.uk/peoplepopulationandcommunity/birthsdeathsandmarriages/ageing/articles/livinglongerhowourpopulationischangingandwhyitmatters/2018-08-13

Phillips, C (2022) 'Are you and your family prepared for the "Great Wealth Transfer"?' 26 October. URL: firstwealth.co.uk/article/are-you-and-your-family-prepared-for-the-great-wealth-transfer?

Resolution Foundation (2022) 'The UK's wealth gaps have grown to over £1.2 million'. 22 July. URL: resolutionfoundation.org/press-releases/the-uks-wealth-gaps-have-grown-to-over-1-2-million

Retrowow (no date) 'How much did cars cost in the 60s?' URL: retrowow.co.uk/transport/60s/motoring/60s_cars_cost.php

Tomlinson, J (2021) 'Deindustrialisation and "Thatcherism": Moral economy and unintended consequences'. Contemporary British History 35(4). URL: doi.org/10.1080/13619462.2021.1972416

Chapter 7

Bank of England (2025) 'Official Bank rate history'. URL: bankofengland.co.uk/boeapps/database/Bank-Rate.asp

Bolton, P (2012) – see Chapter 6.

Coupland, D (1991) – see Chapter 4.

Mahmoud, A B, Hack-Polay, D et al (2021) 'Who's more vulnerable? A generational investigation of COVID-19 perceptions' effect on organisational citizenship behaviours in the MENA region: Job insecurity, burnout and job satisfaction as mediators'. BMC Public Health 21(1951). URL: doi.org/10.1186/s12889-021-11976-2

Woo, A (2018) 'The forgotten generation: Let's talk about Generation X'. *Forbes*, 14 November. URL: forbes.com/councils/forbesagencycouncil/2018/11/14/the-forgotten-generation-lets-talk-about-generation-x

Chapter 8

Bolton, P (2024) 'Student loan statistics'. House of Commons Library, 5 December. URL: commonslibrary.parliament.uk/research-briefings/sn01079

Doherty, F (2025) 'The SuperJam Story'. SuperJam. URL: superjam.co.uk/pages/about

Fink, C (2023) 'The power of participation trophies'. *Psychology Today*, 27 February. URL: psychologytoday.com/gb/blog/changing-minds/202302/the-power-of-participation-trophies

Goorin, J & Baumgarten, R (2023) 'Insights and innovation: For Gen Z, identity is what they make it'. Voxmedia, 4 April. URL: voxmedia.com/2023/4/4/23669479/for-gen-z-identity-is-what-they-make-it

Gov.uk (2022) 'Academic year 2019/20: Participation measures in higher education'. 17 January. URL: explore-education-statistics.service.gov.uk/find-statistics/participation-measures-in-higher-education/2019-20

Hansard (1989) 'Higher education (age participation rate)'. Vol 152, 2 May. URL: hansard.parliament.uk/Commons/1989-05-02/debates/9e2742c5-9075-434d-8d43-9f562d0a2516/HigherEducation%28AgeParticipationRate%29

Howe, N & Strauss, W (2009) *Millennials Rising: The next great generation*. Knopf Doubleday.

Kuzmenko, E (2023) 'Stripe's founders: The story of Collison brothers who changed online payments forever'. Kitrum, 4 April. URL: kitrum.com/blog/stripe-founders-the-story-of-collison-brothers

Legislation.gov.uk (2025a) 'Higher Education Act 2004'. The National Archives. URL: legislation.gov.uk/ukpga/2004/8/contents

Legislation.gov.uk (2025b) 'Higher Education and Skills Act 2008'. The National Archives. URL: legislation.gov.uk/ukpga/2008/25/contents

Legislation.gov.uk (2025c) 'Teaching and Higher Education Act 1998'. The National Archives. URL: legislation.gov.uk/ukpga/1998/30/contents

Mahmoud & Hack-Polay (2021) – see Chapter 7.

Roos, J & Strand, B (2021) 'The conundrum of participation trophies in youth sports'. PHE America, 18 October. URL: pheamerica.org/2021/the-conundrum-of-participation-trophies-in-youth-sports

Rübner Jørgensen, C & Wyness, M (2021) *Kid Power, Inequalities and Intergenerational Relations*. Anthem Press.

Sinek, S (2016) 'Millennials in the workplace'. YouTube, 30 December. URL: youtube.com/watch?v=vudaAYx2IcE

Stein, J (2013) 'Millennials: The me me me generation'. *Time*, 20 May. URL: time.com/247/millennials-the-me-me-me-generation

Chapter 9

Ackerman, N (2024) 'Never mind the side hustle – these Gen Zers are the real deal'. *The Times*, 2 April. URL: thetimes.com/business-money/entrepreneurs/article/gen-z-young-founders-company-directors-enterprise-network-xqbfgz3jg

Akshay Ruparelia. URL: akshayruparelia.com

Ben Towers. URL: bentowers.com

Butler, S (2024) 'Secondhand fashion seller Vinted moves into profit after 61% sales rise'. *The Guardian*, 29 April. URL: theguardian.com/business/2024/apr/29/secondhand-fashion-seller-vinted-profit-sales-rise-depop-realreal

De Gayardon, A, Callender, C et al (2018) 'Graduate indebtedness: Its perceived effects on behaviour and life choices – a literature review'. Centre for Global Higher Education, University of Oxford. URL: ora.ox.ac.uk/objects/uuid%3A155a0c09-7c6b-4d05-92c0-a32ac3e952b9

Deloitte (2023) 'Mental Health Today: A deep dive based on the 2023 Gen Z and Millennial Survey'. URL: deloitte.com/content/dam/Deloitte/global/Documents/deloitte-2023-genz-millennial-survey-mental-health.pdf

HESA (2024) 'Higher Education Student Statistics: UK, 2022/23 – student numbers and characteristics'. 8 August. URL: hesa.ac.uk/news/08-08-2024/sb269-higher-education-student-statistics/numbers

Jolly, N (2024) '"Experiences over possessions": Gen Z study finds a generation living for today'. Mumbrella, 1 March. URL: mumbrella.com.au/experiences-over-possessions-gen-z-study-finds-a-generation-living-for-today-817711

Mark, G (2023) *Attention Span: A groundbreaking way to restore balance, happiness and productivity*. Hanover Square Press.

Relate (2022) '"Milestone anxiety" on the rise among millennials and Gen Z'. URL: relate.org.uk/get-help/milestone-anxiety-rise-among-millennials-and-gen-z

Ricardo, D (2024) 'Apprenticeships in the UK: Key trends and data for 2023/2024'. Starting Point, 10 June. URL: mystartingpoint.co.uk/uk-apprenticeship-data

Richardson, N & Antonello, M (2023) 'People at work 2023: A global workforce view'. ADP Research, 18 April. URL: adpresearch.com/assets/people-at-work-2023-a-global-workforce-view

Scott, H (2024) 'Fifteen ways the UK education system is failing children'. Edge Media, 18 May. URL: edge.media/ways-the-uk-education-system-is-failing-children

Seemiller, C & Grace, M (2018) *Generation Z: A century in the making*. Routledge.

Chapter 10

Dwyer, S (2025) 'The Gen Alpha workplace: Adapting office environments for a new generation'. *Work Design Magazine*, 19 February. URL: workdesign.com/2025/02/the-generation-alpha-workplace

Forbes (2024) 'Profile: Ryan Kaji'. 28 October. URL: forbes.com/profile/ryan-kaji

Leyts, M (2024) 'What are the characteristics of Generation Alpha'. Generation ZAlpha, 3 July. URL: generationzalpha.com/blog/what-are-the-characteristics-of-generation-alpha

Lurie Children's Hospital of Chicago (2024) 'Millennial parenting statistics: Navigating modern parenthood in today's world'. Lurie Children's, 11 January. URL: luriechildrens.org/en/blog/millennial-parenting-statistics

McCrindle, M & Fell, A (2021) *Generation Alpha: Understanding our children and helping them thrive*. Headline Home.

Vo, S & Webb, L (2024) 'Support for neurodivergent children and young people'. *UK Parliament Post*, 733 24 October. URL: researchbriefings.files.parliament.uk/documents/POST-PN-0733/POST-PN-0733.pdf

Weal, S, Duncan, P et al (2025) 'How Covid changed children in Britain'. *The Guardian*, 18 March. URL: theguardian.com/uk-news/2025/mar/18/how-covid-changed-children-britain

Chapter 11

Kemp, S (2024) – see Chapter 3.

NRS (2016) 'Social grade'. URL: nrs.co.uk/nrs-print/lifestyle-and-classification-data/social-grade

Chapter 12

Young, K (2025) '98% of Gen Z own a smartphone'. GWI. URL: gwi.com/blog/98-percent-of-gen-z-own-a-smartphone

Chapter 13

Three UK (2023) 'Call me maybe? Three UK reveals the nation's phone habits, likes and dislikes'. 3 April. URL: www.threemediacentre.co.uk/content/call-me-maybe-three-uk-reveals-the-nations-phone-habits-likes-and-dislikes

Chapter 14

Haidt, J (2024) – see Chapter 4.

Positive Social. URL: positivesocial.org.uk

Chapter 15

Bolton, P (2025) – see Chapter 4.

Children's Commissioner (2025) 'Most headteachers restrict mobile phones in school hours – but major new survey shows online harms still among their biggest concerns'. 10 April. URL: childrenscommissioner.gov.uk/statement/ press-notice-most-headteachers-restrict-mobile-phones-in-school-hours-but-major-new-survey-shows-online-harms-still-among-their-biggest-concerns

Chapter 16

Silverton, K (2024) *There's Still No Such Thing as Naughty.* Bonnier Books.

Chapter 18

Arturi, T (2024) 'Multigenerational keys to workplace happiness: Insights and strategies'. *Forbes,* 19 November. URL: forbes.com/councils/ forbescoachescouncil/2024/11/19/multigenerational-keys-to-workplace-happiness-insights-and-strategies/

Grant, K, Egdell, V & Vincent, D (2021) 'Young people's expectations of work and the readiness of the workplace for young people: Two sides of the same coin?' Northumbria University and Edinburgh Napier University. URL: researchportal.northumbria.ac.uk/ws/portalfiles/ portal/51511115/RIG_Report_FINAL_Grant_etal_4May21. pdf

Office for National Statistics (2022) 'People aged 65 years and over in employment, UK: January to March 2022 to April to June 2022'. 12 September. URL: ons.gov.uk/employmentandlabourmarket/ peopleinwork/employmentandemployeetypes/ articles/peopleaged65yearsandoverinemploymentuk/ januarytomarch2022toapriltojune2022

Chapter 19

Inqqa AI. URL: inqqa.ai

Chapter 20

Butler, S (2019) *Manage the Gap: Achieving success with intergenerational teams.* Rethink Press.

Deloitte (2024) '2024 Gen Z and Millennial Survey: Living and working with purpose in a transforming world'. URL: deloitte.com/global/en/issues/work/content/genz-millennialsurvey.html

Focardi, R (2021) *Reframing Generational Stereotypes: Embrace age diversity, build mutual understanding and foster collaboration to drive positive change.* McGraw Hill.

Mao, Y, Quan, J et al (2021) 'The differential implications of employee narcissism for radical versus incremental creativity: A self-affirmation perspective'. *Journal of Organizational Behavior* 42(7). URL: doi.org/10.1002/job.2540

Simply HR (2025) 'The benefits of multigenerational training: Boosting employee engagement across ages'. 23 January. URL: simplyhrinc.com/the-benefits-of-multi-generational-training-boosting-employee-engagement-across-ages

Singh, U & Weimar, D (2017) 'Empowerment among generations'. *German Journal of Human Resource Management* 31(4). URL: journals.sagepub.com/doi/abs/10.1177/2397002217719864

Chapter 21

Alda, A (2017) *If I Understood You, Would I Have This Look on My Face? My adventures in the art and science of relating and communicating.* Penguin Random House.

Haidt, J (2024) – see Chapter 4.

Wright, M (2021) 'How every child can thrive by five'. TED and Minderoo Foundation. URL: ted.com/talks/molly_wright_how_every_child_can_thrive_by_five

Thanks and acknowledgements

When started writing this book, I never realised how much help I would need, so I'm hugely grateful to all those who have supported me. I'm hugely appreciative to all the authors of the numerous books I read while researching this one – they taught me so much and I now know how much work it takes!

There are so many people who been on this exciting and long journey with me, so my first thanks go to all the team at the Right Book Company, Sue, Paul, Caroline, Bev, Nick, Andrew and Natalia for all their expertise and talent. To all my podcast guests, especially those who let me quote them in this book, Lynda, Anthony, Mark, Paul and Claudette. To Russ, Lis, Fi, Carole, David and Shelley – I've really appreciated your guidance and encouragement. Thanks also to Deborah, for writing the foreword.

Finally, to my very patient wife Donna, my family and friends across all generations, who have been incredibly supportive throughout the process and listened to me talking about generations constantly over the last five or more years since I decided to embark on this adventure - thank you all so much.

About the author

Alastair Greener is a communications consultant specialising in generational communication. Through his engaging talks and consultancy, he empowers businesses to create cohesive, productive teams while fostering stronger business relationships through effective communication across generations.

A former TV presenter, Alastair is the founder of Present Yourself, which helps organisations communicate more effectively on screen, on stage or online. He is a Fellow of the Professional Speaking Association and has served on the board for three years, becoming the National President in 2025.

He has a wealth of experience in the global hospitality and entertainment industries, and brings the valuable lessons learned from interacting with a wide variety of people to his communications work.

Alastair is married to Donna and has lived in Wiltshire for over 25 years. Having spent many years travelling for his job, he still loves to be on the move and at times delivers lectures on the cruise ships where he once worked.